T0171619

To cease or not to cease:

SPIRITUAL GIFTS TODAY?

Mark Anderson

WESTBOW
PRESS
A DIVISION OF THOMAS NELSON

ISBN: 978-1-4497-5354-2 (sc)
Library of Congress Control Number: 2012909373

WestBow Press books may be ordered through booksellers or by contacting:
WestBow Press - A Division of Thomas Nelson
1663 Liberty Drive, Bloomington, IN 47403
www.westbowpress.com: 1-(866) 928-1240

-"Unless otherwise indicated all Scripture quotations are from The Holy Bible, English Standard Version® (ESV®), copyright © 2001 by Crossway, a publishing ministry of Good News Publishers. Used by permission. All rights reserved."
-"Scripture taken from the NEW AMERICAN STANDARD BIBLE®, Copyright © 1960,1962,1963,1968,1971,1972,1973,1975,1977,1995 by The Lockman Foundation. Used by permission."
-Scripture quotations marked (NLT) are taken from the Holy Bible, New Living Translation, copyright © 1996, 2004, 2007 by Tyndale House Foundation. Used by permission of Tyndale House Publishers, Inc., Carol Stream, Illinois 60188. All rights reserved.
-Scripture quotations marked (NIV) are taken from the Holy Bible, New International Version®, NIV®. Copyright © 1973, 1978, 1984, 2011 by Biblica, Inc.™ Used by permission of Zondervan. All rights reserved worldwide. www.zondervan.com.
-The "NIV" and "New International Version" are trademarks registered in the United States Patent and Trademark Office by Biblica, Inc.™

Printed in the United States of America
WestBow Press rev. date: 06/12/12

'He will glorify me' (John 16:14).

Acknowledgements

This project would not have been brought to completion without the help of the following.

My wonderful wife Rosnah for her encouragement and unwavering support in this project.

My father, Gary Anderson for his suggestions and editing.

Michael Ross-Watson for kindly writing the foreword.

Most of all my utmost thanks and gratitude goes to my Lord and Saviour, Jesus Christ for His unfailing love and grace, and for enabling me to write this book.

May His Name be glorified!

Foreword

In 1969 I was filled with the Holy Spirit and began a wonderful journey of walking with God in the realm of the Spirit. As I have read Mark Anderson's book on the gifts of the Spirit and his clear presentation of the truth of God's Word it has blessed me.

As missionaries in a dark corner of Indonesia we were often faced with demonic powers and great darkness, and we were so grateful to God for the gifts of the Holy Spirit that strengthened us and enabled us to come through in victory. When the darkness was so dark and the oppression so strong we would often retreat to our room and pray in tongues until the oppression lifted. It was so often a word of knowledge supernaturally imparted to our spirit that directed us. Clear prophetic words gave us vision and hope in difficult situations. We are so grateful for these wonderful Holy Spirit gifts that God has given to make us more effective in our life and service for Him.

Mark brings a very clear scriptural foundation in presenting the gifts of the Holy Spirit and their validity today and he clearly answers from Scripture the arguments of those who reject these wonderful gifts.

In my experience the main reasons why people reject the teaching of Scripture on the gifts of the Holy Spirit being available today is either fear, bad experience or bad teaching. Some people are afraid of the supernatural. Others have had bad experience of people who were either not a good testimony or displayed unbiblical excesses. Others have been taught wrongly and have embraced that teaching without checking the Scriptures for themselves.

We read in the book of Acts that the believers in Berea were more noble-minded because they received the word with great eagerness, examining the Scriptures daily, to see whether these things were true (Acts 17:11). I would encourage you to read this book with an open mind and with an open Bible, and believe that as you do so you will be blessed and encouraged.

Michael Ross-Watson
Missionary, Bible teacher and friend in Christ

Contents

Introduction

Is there anything new that can be said about the Person and ministry of the Holy Spirit? It seems we are spoiled for choice given the wealth of material that's available. What you will read in the ensuing pages may not be necessarily new, but in fact rather old - around 2000 years actually. With today's changing trends and the emergence of 'seeker sensitive' gatherings, it could be argued that the biblical experience of Spirit empowerment and all that it entails, has been toned down in the name of 'being balanced'.

This book has been written not with the intention of being 'seeker sensitive', but user friendly. Many have had traumatic experiences in zealous church/house-group gatherings that indelibly imprinted them for life. Traumatized 'sheep' have found a safe haven and a sympathetic ear in equally zealous heresy hunters, who see their life's mission in attacking and criticizing (some of it justified) people who are sincerely trying to fulfill the great commission and provide spiritual help. It is my intention that this book will help both the 'traumatized' and 'critics' see, that what has been misused and misrepresented, is in many instances, a sincere desire to cultivate normal New Testament Christianity. The church needs encouragement and edification, and it is my prayer that the traumatized will recover their desire to encounter the dynamic Spirit and become the people God has called them to be. Equally as enthusiasts for the fulness of the Holy Spirit, I pray that we will be sensitive in helping others enjoy God's gracious provision for effective Christian service.

My background is Pentecostal and I will always defend the experience of the fulness of the Spirit. However, as a lover of Scripture, I owe it to good hermeneutical[1] practice to present as accurately as possible, a scriptural understanding of the ministry of the Holy Spirit. While I won't compromise on the power and gifts of the Spirit, my presentation on some points may conflict with traditional Pentecostal doctrine. Inevitably I might ruffle a few charismatic feathers, but my plea is for the reader to read what follows with an open mind and not through the lens of tradition and culture. It is my hope that this book will convey the necessity of the gifts of the Spirit and the pressing need to defend and articulate their relevance and importance, as we seek to fulfil the Great Commission of reaching the lost and making disciples. Barriers built upon fear and fanaticism continue to exist between traditional evangelicals and Pentecostals, and so I pray this book will in some small way help build the bridge of mutual learning and respect.

A growing number of churches, especially Pentecostal, are seeing God's power manifesting in their gatherings. People are speaking in other tongues, prophesying and praying for the sick. Many leave healed and restored and numerous testify to being strengthened and encouraged through receiving prophecies. Such phenomena are not new, but through the media of the internet and Christian Television,[2]

---

1   Hermeneutics is the science of interpreting scripture.
2   I'm not inferring that all purported manifestations of the Spirit on Christian Television are credible.

many are being exposed to the manifestations of the Holy Spirit for the first time. Where previous fear of church reprisals prevented curious church members from visiting such gatherings, they now whet their spiritual appetites by watching at a safe distance in the privacy of their homes.

Appetites have been whetted which have led many to experience God for themselves in a new and dynamic way. Lives have been transformed, and once ardent sceptics have now become champions for the Spirit's ministry. Inevitably such gatherings which do not advocate nor allow such ministry, have produced and promoted propaganda to arouse suspicion, and dissuade loyal members from exploring further. Such understandable motivation may arise from insecurity or ignorance, hence the reason for this book.

It is my intention and hope that this book will accurately inform what the Bible says about these controversial gifts, but when reading, I again would implore the reader to assess and evaluate this material with an open mind. It is presupposed that the reader has some knowledge of the gifts of the Spirit as it is not within the scope of this book to define them at length and discuss their usage.[3] As a Pentecostal, I will be the first to admit that some Pentecostal groupings, like other denominations, have faults and excesses.

As this book is about the Spirit's manifestations, it is only proper that I begin by introducing the Person of the Holy Spirit. Then, I will define cessationism and scrutinize four texts that are commonly used for its justification. The remainder of the book will be devoted to addressing common fallacies which many espouse to bolster their belief in cessationism,

---

3   An excellent resource is Storms, Sam. *The Beginner's Guide to Spiritual Gifts*. Ventura: Regal Books, 2002.

and to suggest a way forward. My intention is twofold. Firstly that the layperson will be equipped to scripturally articulate the defence and necessity of the Spirit's manifestations today and secondly, that the cessationist will see that God's power and gifts are not consigned to the apostolic era, but are vital in our evangelistic efforts and in the preparation of the bride of Christ to meet her Bridegroom at that Last day. In my writing I will use the terms 'manifestations', and 'gifts of the Spirit' interchangeably.

A Question of Identity

For many the problem stems from childhood. Images of a long-haired, bearded man with a little half-moon above His head are indelibly imprinted on our minds. Jesus the man poses no problem for our understanding. While we may have not seen an illustrator's depiction of God the Father, we have no difficulty in visualizing His being, despite not attributing to Him shape or form. Not so the Holy Spirit. The Holy Spirit creates difficulty for many. Is He wind or water; liquid or light - or perhaps some kind of invisible force or influence?

Two Common Errors

In relation to the Holy Spirit's identity, two common misconceptions are held. Firstly, some regard Him as an influence or concept as opposed to being a distinct Person. Secondly, while many understand Him to be significant in their Christian beliefs, He is subconsciously afforded an inferior position to God the Father and Jesus. Indicative of these errors is the spoken reference of many believers who refer to the Holy Spirit as an 'it'.

He is a Person

What makes a person a person? To be a person requires having a personality which implies the existence of certain attributes. A personality houses intellect, emotion and volition, and all three are characteristic of the Holy Spirit.

The Holy Spirit has *intellect* - He knows and understands things.

> *'For who knows a person's thoughts except the spirit of that person, which is in him? So also no one comprehends the thoughts of God except the Spirit of God'* (1 Corinthians 2:11).

Not only does the Holy Spirit possess intellect, but He also has feelings and emotions. He engages in the highest form of emotion - *love.*

> *'I appeal to you, brothers, by our Lord Jesus Christ and by the love of the Spirit, to strive together with me in your prayers to God on my behalf'* (Romans 15:30).

The Holy Spirit loves and also demonstrates empathy with human weakness and frailty.

> *'Likewise the Spirit helps us in our weakness. For we do not know what to pray for as we ought, but the Spirit himself intercedes for us with groanings too deep for words'* (Romans 8:26).

Here is love and empathy in action; when we don't feel like praying, when words fail us, when words are at times inadequate to express our heart-felt emotions to God, the Holy Spirit is faithful to help us and empower us in our prayer life. He is only too willing to help.

The Holy Spirit is easily grieved.

> *'And do not grieve the Holy Spirit of God, by whom you were sealed for the day of redemption'* (Ephesians 4:30).

He can be grieved. How is this possible?

Consider the context of Ephesians 4:30. This Scripture is sandwiched between verses 29 and 31 which speak of how the believer grieves God's Spirit.

> *'Let no corrupting talk come out of your mouths, but only such as is good for building up, as fits the occasion, that it may give grace to those who hear'* (Ephesians 4:29).

> *'Let all bitterness and wrath and anger and clamor and slander be put away from you, along with all malice'* (Ephesians 4:31).

The *words* we speak and the *attitudes* we hold can be offensive to the Holy Spirit and grieve Him. When He is grieved, He withdraws the sense of His presence. Conversely, if we walk in love, minister grace and demonstrate Christ-likeness, we can create a climate that is conducive for the Holy Spirit to minister amongst the body of Christ. When His presence is welcomed and sought after, we can expect His ministry in our gatherings.

The Holy Spirit has feelings, possesses intellect and has the ability to make decisions. In 1 Corinthians 12:4-11 we see His decision-making faculties demonstrated. This passage shows the Holy Spirit deciding which gifts are given to each member of the body of Christ. He makes independent choices in imparting different gifts to different believers on different occasions. It is the Spirit who decides who gets what and when.

> '*All these are empowered by one and the same Spirit, who apportions to each one individually as he wills*' (1 Corinthians 12:11).

He is God

Throughout Scripture we read of the Spirit speaking, guiding, filling, restricting, working, convicting and comforting. Only an active person is capable of engaging in such activities. An influence or force cannot. The Holy Spirit is a *person*. In Scripture He is referred to with the pronoun 'He'. However He is not just *any* person - He is God.

Concerning water baptism we read:

> '*Go therefore and make disciples of all nations, baptizing them in the name of the Father and of the Son and of the Holy Spirit*' (Matthew 28:19).

Notice that the Holy Spirit is equal with God the Father and God the Son. Consider the chilling deaths of Ananias and Sapphira. Landowners within the church were selling land and bringing the proceeds to the Apostles, who in turn distributed to those in need. Ananias and Sapphira having sold a piece of land, kept part of the proceeds and brought the remainder to the apostles. They were quite within their rights to keep a portion for themselves. Their sin was to deceitfully inform the apostles that they had given them all the proceeds from the sale, while not disclosing the fact that they had kept some for themselves.

> '*But a man named Ananias, with his wife Sapphira, sold a piece of property, and with his wife's knowledge he kept back for himself some of the proceeds and brought only a part of it and laid it at the apostles' feet.*

> *But Peter said, "Ananias, why has Satan filled your*
> *heart to lie to the Holy Spirit and to keep back for*
> *yourself part of the proceeds of the land?*
> *While it remained unsold, did it not remain your own?*
> *And after it was sold, was it not at your disposal? Why*
> *is it that you have contrived this deed in your heart?*
> *You have not lied to men but to God"'* (Acts 5:1-4).

Notice that Peter told Ananias that he had lied to the *Holy Spirit*. He then reinforces the gravity of this sin by stating that he had lied unto God. Lying to the Holy Spirit is lying to God. Why? The Holy Spirit is God.

He possesses the divine characteristic of omnipresence.

> *'Where shall I go from your Spirit? Or where shall I*
> *flee from your presence? If I ascend to heaven, you are*
> *there! If I make my bed in Sheol, you are there!'*
> (Psalm 139:7-8).

He is referred to as the *eternal* Spirit.

> *'how much more will the blood of Christ, who through*
> *the eternal Spirit offered himself without blemish to*
> *God, purify our conscience from dead works to serve*
> *the living God'* (Hebrews 9:14).

We read of Him throughout Scripture, beginning in Genesis 1 and concluding in Revelation 22. Upon observing His ministry in both the Old and New Testaments, one sees similarities but also significant differences. In the Old Testament, His ministry was limited as relatively few people, namely prophets, priests and kings, had an awareness of the Holy Spirit in their lives. The prophets spoke, however, of a future time when the Holy Spirit would be outpoured for *all* God's people.

> *'And I will give them one heart, and a new spirit I will put within them. I will remove the heart of stone from their flesh and give them a heart of flesh, that they may walk in my statutes and keep my rules and obey them. And they shall be my people, and I will be their God'* (Ezekiel 11:19-20).

> *'And it shall come to pass afterward, that I will pour out my Spirit on all flesh; your sons and your daughters shall prophesy, your old men shall dream dreams, and your young men shall see visions. Even on the male and female servants in those days I will pour out my Spirit'* (Joel 2:28-29).

Joel's prophecy was echoed by Peter who cited its fulfillment on the day of Pentecost - a day which heralded a new era of the relationship between the believer and the Holy Spirit.

The Divine Connection

"God is spirit, and those who worship Him must worship in spirit and truth" (John 4:24) (NASB).

Not only is God love and not only is He light - He is also Spirit. God who is Spirit has saved and called us to a relationship with Him. He seeks a love relationship with each of His children. The first commandment after all, is to *'love the Lord our God with all of our heart, soul and mind'* (Matt. 22:37). God seeks a love relationship with His children. John the Beloved Apostle, reminds his readers that we can only love God, because He first loved us (1 John 4:19). Unlike human relationships, our cultivating intimacy with God takes place not on the natural plane, but through Christ and the Holy Spirit. Both Jesus and the Spirit intercede on behalf of the believer.

> *'Who is to condemn? Christ Jesus is the one who died - more than that, who was raised - who is at the right hand of God, who indeed is interceding for us'* (Romans 8:34).

> *'Likewise the Spirit helps us in our weakness. For we do not know what to pray for as we ought, but the Spirit himself intercedes for us with groanings too deep for words' (v. 26).*

Spirit to spirit

As children of God, we commune with Him in 'spirit and in truth'. Let's unpack the meaning of this phrase. To worship God in Spirit is to recognize that through the Person of the Holy Spirit, time and place no longer matter when it comes to worshipping God. The Holy Spirit transcends all geographical boundaries and limitations. Jesus states in the context of John 4, that worship is not restricted to the temple in Jerusalem or Mount Gerazim. In our modern day setting we could say that communion with God is not confined to a church building (Acts 7:48).

As God is Spirit and worship of Him must be offered in spirit, an individual must therefore be born of the Spirit in order to worship and commune with God. Jesus said to Nicodemeus: *'that which is born of the flesh is flesh, and that which is born of the Spirit is spirit'* (John 3:6).

When one is 'born of the Spirit'[4] the Holy Spirit indwells the human spirit and so one can confidently say that 'Christ is in me' (Col. 1:27).

What does it mean to worship God in truth? In the context of John's gospel, truth essentially refers to embracing and submitting to the word of God.

'So Jesus said to the Jews who had believed in him, "If you abide in my word, you are truly my disciples, and you will know the truth, and the truth will set you free"' (John 8:31-32.)

---

4   Or 'born from above'.

God's word is *absolute truth!*

In His High Priestly prayer, Jesus prayed *'sanctify them in the truth; your word is truth'* (John 17:17).

In John's gospel, truth refers to God's word and also to Jesus Himself.

To worship in truth is to recognize and acknowledge that Jesus is the perfect manifestation of truth - He is truth personified.

Jesus claimed:

> *'I am the way, and the truth, and the life. No one comes to the Father except through me'* (John 14:6).

To summarize, we might say that worshipping God the Father in 'spirit and in truth' is to obey the gospel and surrender totally to Jesus Christ; submit to His word and allow it to instruct and guide us. When we do this, God makes it possible for us to commune with Him through the Holy Spirit.

> *'For through him [Christ – The Truth] we both have access in one Spirit to the Father'* (Ephesians 2:18).

Not Monologue, but Dialogue

When individuals experience 'new birth' they are made alive spiritually with God's life dwelling within them. Having been born of the Spirit, the child of God can now worship and commune with God in 'spirit in and in truth'. God is both loving and relational. His relationship with us is not a monologue but a dialogue. He speaks to His children today.

> *'My sheep hear my voice, and I know them, and they follow me'* (John 10.27).

Not only do we commune with God, but He communes with us. How? In the same way we commune with Him - in 'spirit and in truth'. God speaks to us by the *Holy Spirit* (through scripture, preaching, circumstances, dreams, visions, gifts of the Spirit) and what He says will never come into conflict with or contradict His *truth*. What God speaks will always be in perfect harmony with His Word, the gospel and the teachings of Jesus.

As human beings we have a spirit within us which enables us to commune with God. A debate has raged for years as to whether we are a trichotomy or dichotomy - are we three parts (body, soul and spirit) or two parts (body and soul/ spirit)? It's not within the remit of this book to engage in this debate, other than to say that we have a spirit which makes fellowship with our Father possible.

Consider the following statement by Elihu - one of Job's so called 'comforters':

> *'But it is the spirit in man, the breath of the Almighty, that makes him understand'* (Job 32:8).

Within every person, there is the *human* spirit which through Christ's death and resurrection, makes relationship with God a reality. Some have wrongly concluded that in the case of an unbeliever, the spirit is dead. According, however, to Scripture, the spirit is alive - but not alive towards God, so in that sense one could say that it is dead only towards God. We read that God hardened the spirit of Sihon, King of Hesbon (Deut. 2:30) and Nebuchadnezzar (Dan. 5:20.) As believers in Christ, our spirits are alive because of righteousness.

Dr Wayne Grudem points out:

> 'When Paul says, "Your spirits are alive because of
> righteousness" (Rom. 8:10), he apparently means 'alive
> to God', but he does not imply that our spirits were
> completely 'dead' before, only that they were out of
> fellowship with God and were dead in that sense.[5]

As believers our spirits have been made alive in Christ which
enables us through the Holy Spirit, to worship Him in 'spirit
and in truth'.

We have a Divine connection. As children of God we are
one with Christ through the Holy Spirit. We died with
Christ, were buried with Him through baptism and were
raised with Him to walk in newness of life! (Rom. 6:3-8).

Are you Thirsty?

Jesus said: 'If anyone thirsts, let him come to Me and drink.
He who believes in Me, as the Scripture has said, out of his
heart will flow rivers of living water' (John 7:37-38).

John clarifies that Jesus' statement refers to those who would
receive the Holy Spirit after Jesus was glorified (v. 39).

Jesus made this statement on the last day of the Feast of
Tabernacles. One significant feature of this feast was a water
pouring ceremony, whereby a golden flagon was filled with
water from the pool of Siloam and then carried by the High
Priest who led a procession to the temple. The water was
subsequently poured out before the Lord in remembrance
of His provision of water for Israel in the desert, and also
in looking forward to the Spirit being outpoured in the

5   Grudem, Wayne A. *Systematic theology*. Leicester: Inter-
Varsity Press, 1994, p481.

last days. Images of Ezekiel's life giving river issuing from the temple no doubt would have been in the minds of the observers. When Jesus invited the thirsty to come to Him and drink, they would have been reminded of Isaiah 55:1:

'Come, everyone who thirsts, come to the waters.'

When Jesus gave His invitation to come to Him and drink, He was, in essence, saying that He could supply the waters which Isaiah spoke of.

For those who are spiritually thirsty for God and express their thirst by coming to Jesus to 'drink', they will experience and enjoy the fulness of the Spirit working in them and flowing through them as life giving rivers *from* them to minister to others.

What is Cessationism?

People who don't believe that the nine manifestations of the Spirit outlined in 1 Corinthians 12 are for today are called 'cessationists'. They don't recognize that the Holy Spirit can still manifest Himself through believers in the manner Paul cites, including healing the sick and working miracles by the power of the Holy Spirit; nor do they believe that the gifts of speaking in tongues and prophecy etc are for today. Such people are sincere, but I believe, sincerely wrong. The doctrine they espouse is called 'cessationism'. Its tenets in essence state that gifts such as healing, miracles, prophecy and tongues ceased with the death of the last apostle and the completion of the canon of Scripture; the stated purpose of such gifts, was to help launch the New Testament church and spread the gospel, while providing authenticity and credibility to the apostles. I shall be later discussing four texts used to justify cessationism: 1 Corinthians 13:8-13; Ephesians 2:20-22; Hebrews 1:1-2; 2:3-4.

Cessationism was given credibility by Calvin in his 'Institutes of the Christian Religion'. As a result of the Reformation, the Roman Catholic church was losing large numbers and as a counter measure, set in hand a strategy to attempt to win them back and also gain new members. Cardinal Robert Bellarmine, one of the key figures in the 'Counter Reformation'[6] pointed to the so-called 'supernatural happenings' current at that time within the Roman Catholic church. He said that 'they are necessary for new faith or for extraordinary missionary persuasion' and further stated that 'they are efficacious and sufficient' and that 'they cannot be among the adversaries of the true church[7] and that the true church is among us.'[8] This essentially was tantamount to a challenge issued to the Reformers to produce their own miracles? The gauntlet was thrown down and the Reformers knew they had to respond.

In questioning the Roman Catholic sacrament of 'Extreme Unction'[9] and in particular its tenet stating possible restoration of bodily health after administering it to a sick or dying individual, Calvin wrote:

---

6   The Counter Reformation was a reform movement within the Roman Catholic church in response to the Protestant Reformation.

7   Bellarmine considered the Roman Catholic church to be the only 'true church'.

8   Mullin, Robert Bruce. *Miracles and the Modern Religious Imagination.* New Haven: Yale University Press, 1996, p12.

9   A sacrament of the New Law instituted by Christ to give spiritual aid and comfort and perfect spiritual health, including, if need be, the remission of sins, and also, conditionally, to restore bodily health, to Christians who are seriously ill. 'Catholic Encylopedia' *www.newadvent.org/cathen/05716a.htm*

> *'But the gift of healing disappeared with the other miraculous powers which the Lord was pleased to give for a time, that it might render the new preaching of the gospel for ever wonderful'.*[10]

With this remark from so prominent a theologian, cessationsim was given an air of respectability and this view began to take root and spread. It was later propagated by Benjamin Breckon Warfield - a distinguished theological professor at Princeton Seminary. Warfield documented his views in his book 'Counterfeit Miracles' and his influence is still evident today in many seminaries.

I would suggest that no one honestly reading Scripture, logically concludes that the miraculous power of God is not available to His people today. A plain reading of Scripture would *not* lead one to arrive at this conclusion. To believe in cessationism is not a natural response to the plain reading of the Bible, but ironically requires one to be systematically taught this view.

It has often been said that Pentecostals place too much emphasis on experience and I would agree to a certain extent, but I would also respectfully say that cessationists also appeal to experience. In their experience, healings and miracles are not common and so their absence may have influenced and contributed to the formation of their beliefs. I say this because the Scriptures clearly demonstrate that the manifestation of the Spirit through gifts of healings, miracles, tongues and prophecy etc, will remain until the glorious appearing of our Lord Jesus Christ (1 Cor. 1:7-8).

---

10   *www.spurgeon.org/~phil/calvin/bk4ch19.html.*

I want to clearly stress from the outset that the gifts of the Spirit are subservient to the Word of God and must not take priority or precedence over Scripture. The Holy Spirit who inspired Scripture will always work in harmony with the Word. Both the Spirit and the word of God are called 'Truth' (John 14:17; 17:17) and truth will not contradict itself. However, how can we disregard and ignore such vital tools, used in conjunction with preaching the gospel and teaching the Scriptures so that the lost may be saved and believers edified?

Cessationism's Core

'*Now about spiritual gifts, brothers, I do not want you to be ignorant.*

You know that when you were pagans, somehow or other you were influenced and led astray to mute idols.

Therefore I tell you that no one who is speaking by the Spirit of God says, "Jesus be cursed," and no one can say, "Jesus is Lord," except by the Holy Spirit.

There are different kinds of gifts, but the same Spirit.

There are different kinds of service, but the same Lord.

There are different kinds of working, but the same God works all of them in all men.

Now to each one the manifestation of the Spirit is given for the common good.

To one there is given through the Spirit the message of wisdom, to another the message of knowledge by means of the same Spirit,

to another faith by the same Spirit, to another gifts of healing by that one Spirit,

to another miraculous powers, to another prophecy, to another distinguishing between spirits, to another speaking in different kinds of tongues, and to still another the interpretation of tongues.

*All these are the work of one and the same Spirit, and
he gives them to each one, just as he determines'* (1
Corinthians 12:1-11) (NIV).

Everyone Loves a Present

Think of a gift. What do you see? A small cuboid shape
perhaps, covered with shiny wrapping paper complete
with a bow on top. The gifts of the Holy Spirit aren't gift-
wrapped; rather they are unwrapped and sadly by many,
they are unwanted. They are unwrapped as they must be
held up for scrutiny and testing, (1 Cor. 14:29; 1 Thess.
5:19-21) and unwanted because many resort to picking and
choosing, keeping what they deem relevant and safe, while
discarding the rest. In the Greek text, the word for 'gift' as
in spiritual gifts is 'charisma'. Simply translated it means
'grace-gift'. Though the word charisma is used in passages
such as Romans 12, for the purpose of this study, I shall be
only considering its use in 1 Corinthians 12 and 14.

In 1 Corinthians 12, Paul speaks of the manifestation of the
Spirit being given to each one. In essence the manifestation
is a gift where God reveals Himself in and through His
people. It's important to note that the word 'manifestation'
is in the singular and not plural, so that the focus is placed
upon God the Holy Spirit and not His activity. Cessationism
essentially does not allow God to reveal Himself through
the Holy Spirit in gathered communities of believers, even
though Scripture exhorts us to *desire* Him to do just that
(1 Cor. 14:1). As stated in my introduction, cessationsim
rests essentially on four key texts: 1 Corinthians 13:8-13;
Ephesians 2:20-22; Hebrews 1:1-2; 2:4. Before we examine
these texts, I would again implore the reader to look with
me honestly and objectively at each, discarding preconceived
ideas shaped by experience and religious background.

Manifold Manifestations

An important key in interpreting Scripture, especially when studying the epistles, is looking always at its context. In studying the Spirit's manifestations, one must recognize that the context is the church assembled for worship. Paul makes five references in 1 Corinthians 11 and two in 1 Corinthians 14 of the church coming *together* (1 Cor.11:17, 18, 20, 33-34; 14:23, 26). Why else would the church come together, but for the purpose of worship? Bearing in mind that there are no chapter divisions in Scripture, this worship context continues as Paul introduces 1 Corinthians 12 to address the Spirit's activity in the gathered church.

There are manifold manifestations of the Holy Spirit in the gathered community though it is commonly taught that there are only nine gifts of the Holy Spirit as nine manifestations are listed (1 Cor. 12:1-11). However when we consider Paul's reason for writing to the Corinthians, the notion of only nine manifestations isn't consistent with his intent. The Corinthians richly experienced the Spirit's ministry, but unfortunately became obsessed with one manifestation in particular - tongues. Using the analogy of the human body (1 Cor. 12:12-27) with each believer being likened to a body part, Paul makes the case that 'if the whole body were an eye, where would be the sense of hearing'? (v. 17). His point is, that just as each part of the human body has a function, so does each believer in the church - the body of Christ. Each believer is needed and necessary. The Corinthians' obsession with tongues fostered disorder and confusion in their gatherings, to the extent that outsiders were reluctant to join them (1 Cor. 14:23).

In 1 Corinthians 12, Paul argues the case for diversity in the Spirit's manifestations and introduces them by emphasizing that they are given to 'each one' or 'to another'. Note that he doesn't introduce these manifestations in the format of first, second, third etc as he does later when speaking about offices in the church (cf. 1 Cor. 12:8-11; 28). The emphasis isn't on nine manifestations, but that nine times he writes 'to another'. Upon reading the flow of Paul's appeal, one could almost put 'etc' after the ninth manifestation. Paul is appealing for diversity while the Corinthians are revelling in uniformity in their obsession with tongues. I will point out in a later chapter, that although the gift of tongues was misused, Paul nevertheless prized its value, esteemed it highly and encouraged the believers to utilise it correctly.

In the community gathered for worship, Paul provides instruction in encouraging the church to expect and facilitate the Spirit's ministry as He manifests Himself through each believer.

The Message of Wisdom
Usually this manifestation is defined as being led to know what to do in a particular situation. It is where God supernaturally reveals the solution to a particular problem. God does grant supernatural wisdom to those who recognise their need of it and ask Him (James 1:5). In his letter to the Colossians, Paul prayed that they would experience spiritual wisdom:

> *'And so, from the day we heard, we have not ceased to pray for you, asking that you may be filled with the knowledge of his will in all spiritual wisdom and understanding'* (Colossians 1:9).

Stephen exhibited such wisdom in his encounter with some men from the 'Freedmen Synagogue'. The Holy Spirit inspired his address to them which they could not withstand (Acts 6:9-10). Such wisdom comes by the Holy Spirit, but is this how Paul understands the message of wisdom, or as some versions render it - 'the word of wisdom'? Paul does envisage such insight but this can be better reflected by the term 'governments' or 'administrations' (1 Cor. 12:28). The word translated 'governments' or 'administrations' is 'κυβόρνησις' which can mean 'wise counsels.'[11]

I would suggest that receiving supernatural insight to know what do in a situation, doesn't accurately reflect the idea of 'the message of wisdom'. The use of the definite article places the emphasis on 'the message' as opposed to wisdom itself. Paul doesn't simply cite this manifestation merely as wisdom, but as 'the message of wisdom'.

In 1 Corinthians, wisdom is not to be understood as merely knowing what to do in a given situation or about receiving insight.

The Corinthian church was influenced by Greek culture and way of thinking, and it is here where we must begin in understanding what wisdom meant to Paul in his letter. To the Greeks, wisdom was a philosophy - a worldview that made sense out of life. Wisdom influenced choices

---

11   *www.blueletterbible.org/lang/lexicon/lexicon. cfm?Strongs=G2941&t=KJV.*

and decision-making. However, there were many different philosophies and worldviews propagated and defended by skilled orators and debaters. The Greeks loved to listen to the rhetoric of such speakers (1 Cor. 1:20) and hear their 'words of wisdom'[12] which inevitably resulted in favouritism. This trait spilled over into the Corinthian church creating factions, with some following Paul, some favouring Peter while others claimed Apollos (vv. 10-13). Paul's solution to this over-dependence on human wisdom is to demonstrate that the message of the cross, is God's wisdom.

> *'For the word of the cross is folly to those who are perishing, but to us who are being saved it is the power of God'* (1 Corinthians 1:18).

> *'but we preach Christ crucified, a stumbling block to Jews and folly to Gentiles, but to those who are called, both Jews and Greeks, Christ the power of God and the wisdom of God'* (vv. 23-24).

In verse 18 'the word of the cross' is the message of the cross. Paul restates this in verses 23 and 24 using the term 'the wisdom of God' as it relates to him preaching Christ crucified - in other words the message of the cross.

Paul called the message of the cross the wisdom of God and stated that he preached it *'not in plausible words of wisdom, but in demonstration of the Spirit and of power'* (1 Cor. 2:4).

'Plausible words of wisdom' is a reference to the rhetoric of the Greco-Roman debaters and orators and it is important

---

12   Literally means 'wisdom of words'. Greeks were enamored with oratory skill.

to understand how Paul contrasts it with the message of the cross - the wisdom of God.

> '*Yet we do speak wisdom among those who are mature; a wisdom, however, not of this age nor of the rulers of this age, who are passing away; but we speak God's wisdom in a mystery, the hidden wisdom which God predestined before the ages to our glory*' (1 Corinthians 2:6-7) (NASB).

This hidden wisdom is God's plan of redemption which none of the earthly rulers were able to comprehend.

> '*None of the rulers of this age understood this, for if they had, they would not have crucified the Lord of glory*' (v. 8).

When Paul preached the cross, he preached the wisdom of God in a mystery. Logically this means that when Paul was preaching, he was speaking words conveying the message of the wisdom of God. I would respectfully suggest that the manifestation known as 'the message of wisdom' is the preaching of the cross which can appear as foolishness to the logical, rational mind (1 Cor. 1:18).

The Message of Knowledge

The traditional Pentecostal and charismatic understanding of this manifestation, is that the Spirit discloses information about persons or circumstances which are unknown to the individual through whom this gift is manifested. A common scenario where this understanding occurs typically plays out like this: 'God is showing me that there is a man here called John, you have been a believer for three months and you have to make an important decision by next Tuesday'.

Happenings like this occur frequently in many gatherings today and while many are proven to be accurate, others are not, and some can be vague and exhibit a mixture of truth and error.

Is this how Paul and the Corinthians understood this manifestation called 'the message of knowledge'? While not being in any way dogmatic, I would like to suggest a possible alternative interpretation. Scripture does not define the meaning of this gift and so it's important that we begin in 1 Corinthians to help us in our quest. Pentecostal Bible teacher, Donald Gee points out that *'we are to look for the word of knowledge as one of the gifts of the Spirit operating in close relationship with other members of the body of Christ."*[13] Wisdom and knowledge in the Corinthian epistle are very closely related. When one thinks of knowledge, one thinks of knowing.

'For who among men knows the thoughts of a man except the spirit of the man which is in him? Even so the thoughts of God no one knows except the Spirit of God. Now we have received, not the spirit of the world, but the Spirit who is from God, so that we may know the things freely given to us by God' (1 Corinthians 2:11-12) (NASB).

The fact that this manifestation is referred to as the 'logos' or 'message of knowledge', suggests it is a gift which is tied to preaching. Paul states that within the Law of Moses is *'the embodiment of knowledge and truth'* (Rom.2:20). Given that the Law forms part of the Old Testament Scriptures, one can confidently assert that the Scriptures are the embodiment

---

13   Gee, Donald. *Concerning Spiritual Gifts.* Springfield: Gospel Publishing House, 1980, p134. Used by permission.

of knowledge and truth. Jesus reaffirmed this when He said *'Your word is truth!'* (John 17:17).

> *'Now, brothers, if I come to you speaking in tongues,*
> *how will I benefit you unless I bring you some revelation*
> *or knowledge or prophecy or teaching?'*
> (1 Corinthians 14:6).

*P*aul uses two parallel pairs in the above Scripture. Revelation parallels with prophecy while knowledge parallels with teaching.

The message of knowledge not only is tied to preaching, but in particular is an unveiling of the truth of the scriptures by the Holy Spirit. While not being dogmatic, it would appear that there is a strong case to suggest that the 'message of knowledge' is or complements the teaching of the Scriptures.

Consider 1 Corinthians 8 where Paul addressed the eating of meat which had been sacrificed to idols. Essentially this matter related to one's conscience and scruples. The issue was whether or not a believer could eat meat which had been sacrificed to an idol. For some believers this meat was tainted as it had been sacrificed to an idol and so was unclean, and not fit for consumption. Paul describes such believers as 'weak'[14] (1 Cor. 8:7-12).

Others viewed matters differently. To them there was but only one God who created all things. As there was only one God, (1 Cor. 8:4-6) then there were no gods behind man-made idols, and so meat which was offered, was to non entities and therefore meaningless. Paul described believers who had this view as having 'knowledge' (v. 7) as they could

---

14   The term 'weak' is used to describe their conscience.

eat such meat without feeling any sense of condemnation. It was 'knowledge' which enabled some believers to have freedom to eat such meat. Note Paul's use of the word 'know' in 1 Corinthians 8:4:

> *'Therefore, as to the eating of food offered to idols, we know that "an idol has no real existence" and that "there is no God but one."'*

It was 'knowledge' which enabled Paul and others to know that there was only one God and that an idol was nothing. Given the context of 1 Corinthians 12 where the 'message of knowledge' is a manifestation of the Spirit, it is probable that Paul's use of knowledge in 1 Corinthians 8 is knowledge which is revealed by the Holy Spirit. I would propose that knowledge is the revealing of truth by the Holy Spirit. The revealing of such truth in 1 Corinthians 8 brought liberty. Jesus Himself said that if *'you continue in My word … you will know the truth and the truth will make you free'* (John 8:32) (NASB). When Paul wrote his first epistle to Timothy, he expressed that it was God's desire that all people be saved and *'come to the knowledge of the truth'* (1 Tim. 2:4). Clearly this is the truth of salvation revealed by the Holy Spirit. In this second letter, Paul wrote of those who were always learning and *'never able to arrive at a knowledge of the truth'* (2 Tim. 3:7). Again it is apparent that there is natural knowledge (acquiring of facts, figures etc through learning) and quite a different kind of knowledge which is truth revealed by the Holy Spirit.

'Knowledge' in 1 Corinthians 8 and 14, is a revealing of truth by the Holy Spirit which produces liberty and growth in the believer's spiritual walk. Paul does, however, affirm that 'knowledge puffs up'[15] whereas 'love builds up' (1 Cor. 8:1). He stresses the importance of choosing love over liberty and alludes to this again in 1 Corinthians 13:2. Given that this manifestation like wisdom is referred to as 'the message of knowledge', it is possible that it is connected with a teaching ministry. Teachers impart the truth of Scripture and often receive fresh insights in their own study and preparation.

Perhaps the purpose of this manifestation of the Spirit is to give insight into the Scriptures, and then enable such insight and truth to be communicated to the assembled church. Donald Gee in his book 'Concerning Spiritual Gifts' states that *'the word of knowledge is a teaching gift in the church'*.[16]

What then are we to make of the traditional Pentecostal interpretation of this gift where one supernaturally receives details about a person or situation? This is a valid gift with a scriptural precedent. If the interpretation of 'the message of knowledge' which I am proposing is accurate, then the traditional Pentecostal view would come under what Paul referred to as a 'revelation' (1 Cor. 14:6). Such revelation is often expressed through the gift of prophecy. Consider 1 Corinthians 14: 24-25:

> *'But if all prophesy, and an unbeliever or outsider enters, he is convicted by all, he is called to account by all, the secrets of his heart are disclosed, and so, falling on his face, he will worship God and declare that God is really among you.'*

---

15   It is not knowledge per se that 'puffs up' but ones attitude to knowledge.

16   Gee, Donald. *Concerning Spiritual Gifts*. Springfield: Gospel Publishing House, 1980, p134. Used by permission.

The secrets of one's heart can be disclosed through the gift of prophecy, just as the secrets of the Samaritan woman were disclosed by Jesus. Her response was: *'Sir, I perceive that you are a prophet'* (John 4:19). Before Jesus was crucified, in their mocking, the soldiers blindfolded Him while one struck Him on the face. They demanded Jesus to tell them which one of them had struck Him. Note how they worded their demand: *'Prophesy! Who is it that struck you?'* (Luke 22:64).

I would respectfully suggest that prophesying is speaking forth a *revelation* while a genuine teaching gift (1 Cor. 12:28) is communicating *knowledge* which has been imparted and illuminated by the Holy Spirit.

In summary both 'wisdom' and 'knowledge' are described as being messages. The message of wisdom is the preaching of the cross and God's plan of redemption, and matters related to them. Knowledge is perhaps more akin to preaching and teaching. Colossians 2:3 states that in Christ *'are hidden all the treasures of wisdom and knowledge.'* Paul stated this so that the Colossians should not be deluded with *'plausible arguments'* (Col. 2:4). In wisdom and knowledge there is exhortation and exposition sprinkled with scriptural insights revealed by the Spirit. If my proposed interpretation of 'the message of wisdom' and 'message of knowledge' is accurate, then it would be extremely difficult to find anyone who could credibly suggest that these two gifts are neither not for, nor happening today. That being the case, what authority then has anyone to exclude the remaining seven gifts and relegate them to the past with no further use?

It's important to remember that when Paul writes about spiritual gifts, he does so in the context of the community gathered for worship. Many believers today, through the influence of church tradition and culture, equate worship with singing only. Minds have been shaped by sentiment, conditioned by culture and influenced by tradition, creating a distorted understanding of worship. Under the umbrella of worship there is a place for singing, music and hand clapping, but worship also includes prayer and preaching. Given the context in which Paul writes, it is reasonable to conclude that the worshipping church will include the preaching of the Scriptures, in both evangelistic (message of wisdom) and teaching (message of knowledge) capacities.

Faith

Faith pleases God (Heb. 11:6). It is an absolute belief in Him and a trusting acceptance of His will. As believers, we already have, and continue to exercise faith in Christ's atoning sacrifice on the cross for our salvation. This aspect of faith could be called 'saving faith'. When we as believers approach God in prayer, we exercise faith by believing that God hears and answers our petitions. But here Paul cites faith as a manifestation of the Spirit. It is a different expression of faith as it is given sovereignly by the Spirit to those whom He wills. Faith here is a gift which grants the recipient *unwavering assurance* that God is about do something supernaturally. Peter displayed a gift of faith in the raising of Dorcas from the dead (Acts 9:36-41). When one is given a *gift* of faith, doubt does not enter into the equation. This aspect of faith could be called 'mountain moving faith'.

Hear the words of Jesus:

> *'For truly, I say to you, if you have faith like a grain of mustard seed, you will say to this mountain, "Move from here to there," and it will move, and nothing will be impossible for you'* (Matthew 17:20).

An example of such unwavering faith is found in Elijah's confrontation on Mount Carmel with the prophets of Baal. Elijah threw down the gauntlet:

> *'How long will you go limping between two different opinions? If the LORD is God, follow him; but if Baal, then follow him'* (1 Kings 18:21).

Elijah then instructs the prophets of Baal to kill a bullock; cut it in pieces and place them on some wood. They are to then call out to Baal for fire to consume their offering. From morning until noon they cry out to Baal, and some even leap onto the altar, but to no avail. Elijah adds to their humiliation by mocking them:

> *'Cry aloud, for he is a god. Either he is musing, or he is relieving himself, or he is on a journey, or perhaps he is asleep and must be awakened'* (v. 27).

When evening came it was Elijah's turn. He killed a bullock, cut it in pieces and placed them on an altar. He then commanded four barrels to be filled with water which was to be poured onto the sacrifice. He asked for the barrels to be refilled and poured onto the sacrifice three times. The very trench around the altar was filled with water. This was quite an act of faith in itself, given there was drought in the land and water was scarce. Elijah then called out to God and then *'the fire of the LORD fell and consumed the burnt offering and the wood and the stones and the dust, and licked up the water that was in the trench'* (v. 38).

Elijah possessed a faith in this event that clearly was supernatural. What a contrast with the next chapter in Elijah's life when he plunged into depression (1 Kings 19:4) following a death threat issued from Jezebel. We should however take comfort, because even though Elijah was a man *'with a nature like ours'*, (James 5:17) he was used powerfully by God.

It's significant to note that James cites Elijah as an example after writing about faith and healing.

> *'Is anyone among you sick? Let him call for the elders of the church, and let them pray over him, anointing him with oil in the name of the Lord. And the prayer of faith will save the one who is sick, and the Lord will raise him up. And if he has committed sins, he will be forgiven'* (James 5: 14-15).

James is not merely referring to a prayer for healing, but rather a unique prayer as denoted by the definite article. It is 'the prayer of faith' which will save the sick. In other words this is a prayer inspired by supernatural faith for the situation at hand.[17]

This kind of faith acts as a catalyst for the next two manifestations - healings and miracles.

Gifts of Healings

Note the wording of this manifestation. In the original it is 'gifts of healings' and not 'the gift of healing' as many today call it. I expand on this in the 'Common Fallacies' chapter. Our God heals today! In the Old Testament, His covenant name was 'Jehovah Rapha' (Ex.15:26). In Scripture, healing is ministered in various ways. The most common method practiced today is prayer accompanied with the 'laying on of

---

17   We should always pray for the sick when required, whether or not we have any awareness of extraordinary faith.

hands'. James writes of healing being administered through the prayer of faith coupled with anointing with oil (James 5:14).

Gifts of healings however are supernaturally and sovereignly given by the Spirit as the need arises. This particular manifestation is in the plural, suggesting that the scope of this gift is diverse. It may be that an individual is effective in this gift for certain specific ailments. Gifts of healings could also relate to the way in which God releases healing. He may heal en masse through prayer without the laying on of hands, or he may heal each person one at a time through the laying on of hands. As believers, we need to recognize that there are gifts of healings and that we can be used by God at anytime, be it only once or many times throughout our lives. It's important to note also that healing in some cases is instantaneous, but is usually gradual.

> *'They will pick up serpents with their hands; and if they drink any deadly poison, it will not hurt them; they will lay their hands on the sick, and they will recover'* (Mark 16:18).

The Working of Miracles

Many definitions of the word 'miracle' exist and one which I feel encapsulates its meaning is that it is 'an extraordinary event manifesting divine intervention in human affairs'. Miracles as recorded in the Bible include God controlling the forces of nature (Jesus rebuking the storm), Jesus raising the dead (Jairus' daughter) and miraculous provision (feeding of the five thousand and the wedding at Cana). Miracles also occur within the realm of healing (Acts 4:22). Regarding the miracle of the man who was crippled from birth in Acts 3:1-10, what is amazing, is not because the use of his feet and legs were restored and strengthened, but he could walk immediately. Professor Elizabeth Hillstrom explains:

> '*The healing of the man who was crippled from birth, recorded in Acts 3:1-10, is even more astounding. In his case, muscles in his feet and legs that were weak from disuse had to be restored and strengthened, and any bone or neural abnormalities had to be repaired. All of this instantaneous replacing and repairing is incredible enough, but if, as the passage suggests, this man had never walked, the miracle is amazing for another reason.*
>
> *Walking upright is a very complicated process, and it takes young children a long time and a good many bumps to learn how to do it. While children are learning to walk, neuronal circuits are apparently formed in motor areas of their brains which can later automatically command the complicated, highly orchestrated muscle movements that are necessary for walking. To enable this man to walk, the Holy Spirit not only had to repair his feet and legs but also had to activate (or create) neurons in the motor areas of the brain and then lay down all the complicated neuronal circuits that are normally established gradually through long hours of practice. Yet when this man rose to his feet, not only did he know how to walk, but he could run and jump as well.*'[18]

The gift of the working of miracles has been given to the body of Christ. Are we seeing miracles like this today? If not, why not?

---

18 Hillstrom, Elizabeth L. *Testing the Spirits*. Downer's Grove: InterVarsity Press, 1995, pp 172-173.

Prophecy

The gift of prophecy enables the believer to bring a word of edification, exhortation and comfort to an individual believer or the assembled church. It begins when God sovereignly and spontaneously reveals a Scripture, thought, picture or impression. Upon communicating such a revelation, the believer is said to be prophesying. Dr Wayne Grudem offers a simple definition for the gift of prophecy as *'telling something that God has spontaneously brought to mind.*[19]*'*

Philip had four daughters who exercised this gift (Acts 21:9). However, the gift of prophecy must not be confused with the office of a prophet. While Philip's daughters prophesied, they are not called prophetesses. Contrast with Agabus who is specifically called a prophet (Acts 21:10). The Scripture is clear that while *'all may prophesy',* (1 Cor. 14:31) *'He gave some...to be prophets' (Eph. 4:11).* Paul valued prophecy very highly and encouraged its use in the church.

Discerning of Spirits

In His Olivet Discourse, Jesus was asked: *'What will be the sign of your coming and the end of the world?'* His response was: *'Take heed that no one deceives you'* (Matt. 24:3-4). Jesus was warning against deception. Shakespeare encapsulated that sentiment when wrote in his play 'The Merchant of Venice', that 'all that glisters is not gold'. Today, there are many heresies and false doctrines, subtly seeking to enslave unsuspecting believers. We live in a day where occultism and New Age philosophies abound. How necessary it is therefore to obey John's command to *'test the spirits to see whether or not they are of God'* (1 John 4:1). In practical terms, this means we are to test or

---

19   Grudem, Wayne A. *Systematic Theology.* Leicester: Inter-Varsity Press, 1994, p1049.

discern every human spirit (every person) who exercises a spiritual gift. It's significant that this gift is mentioned after the gift of prophecy and before the gifts of tongues and interpretation, which would suggest that it is to be employed in the testing and weighing of every utterance purporting to be from God.

Rich Nañez, a Pentecostal pastor, says something is wrong *'if we jettison our minds, confusing every potent inner notion with the voice of God, and thus basing our system of belief on phenomena (real or imagined).'*[20] He adds further wise counsel: *'Test every spirit, prove all things, and by all means, avoid being weird just to be weird, because most often this is simply old-fashioned pride! We need to be careful not to follow every inner unction (especially when self-serving!), not to be bent on seeking signs and wonders, and not to cast off logic and reason as if they were enemies of the supernatural.'*[21]

I would also add that this gift may be used in discerning the presence of an evil spirit at work as in the case of a certain slave girl who had a spirit of divination as recorded in Acts 16:16-18.

> *'As we were going to the place of prayer, we were met by a slave girl who had a spirit of divination and brought her owners much gain by fortune-telling. She followed Paul and us, crying out, "These men are servants of the Most High God, who proclaim to you the way of salvation." And this she kept doing for many days. Paul, having become greatly annoyed, turned and said to the spirit, "I command you in*

---

20   Nañez, Rick M. *Full Gospel Fractured Minds?: A Call to Use God's Gift of the Intellect.* Grand Rapids: Zondervan, 2005, p138.
21   Ibid.

the name of Jesus Christ to come out of her." And it came out that very hour.'

An evil spirit may influence a person's attitude or motivation as well as being the cause of sickness in certain circumstances (Mark 9:25; Luke 13:11).

Tongues

The gift of tongues is essentially a prayer language which offers thanksgiving, praise and prayer to God. When one speaks in tongues, he speaks mysteries in the Spirit and is personally edified. Speaking in tongues in a gathered assembly is manifested in conjunction with the gift of the interpretation of tongues. It should be noted that Scripture does not teach that there are two kinds of tongues. Some view the tongues bestowed at Pentecost (Acts 2:4) as different from the gift of tongues manifested in the church (1 Cor. 12:10). There is only one gift of tongues, but it has two uses (1 Cor. 14:18-19). Firstly, it greatly enhances the believer's personal devotional life as a means of edification, and secondly, with the gift of interpretation of tongues, it edifies the assembled church.

Interpretation of Tongues

This is simply the interpretation of an utterance given to the assembled gathering in an unknown tongue. It's important to note, that it is described as an 'interpretation' and not a 'translation', hence some utterances in tongues may seem longer or shorter than the interpretation. Please note that this gift has nothing to do whatsoever with preaching the gospel in a foreign language.[22] Linguistic knowledge is not involved in the operation of this gift as the interpretation is furnished solely by the manifestation of the Holy Spirit (1 Cor. 12:7).

---

22   Many have testified of hearing the gift of tongues spoken in their own language or dialect.

What's the Time?

Before examining four texts which are used to justify cessationism, I would like to consider 1 Corinthians 1:4-8 which provides the time frame for which one should expect these manifestations to occur.

> 'I give thanks to my God always for you because of the grace of God that was given you in Christ Jesus, that in every way you were enriched in him in all speech and all knowledge - Even as the testimony of Christ was confirmed in you: so that you are not lacking in any spiritual gift, as you wait for the revealing of our Lord Jesus Christ, who will sustain you to the end, guiltless in the day of our Lord Jesus Christ.'

Before probing the above passage, it is necessary to understand something of the Corinthian context. The Corinthians, who had experienced the power of the Spirit in their gatherings, wrongly concluded that they had 'arrived' spiritually speaking. They understood speaking in tongues to be the ultimate mark of spirituality, and this faulty perception influenced much of their theology. To them, speaking in other tongues was the ultimate spiritual experience. It fostered an incorrect understanding as to what it meant to be spiritual and led them to believe they had achieved angelic status.

Paul seeks to encourage them in the exercise of spiritual gifts, while correcting their misconceptions and theology. He begins by thanking God for them and their enriching experience of spiritual gifts such as speech and knowledge. He attributes such enrichment to God's grace and links it to an event in the past - an event where the testimony of Christ was confirmed in them. This was when Paul had preached the gospel to them resulting in their conversion and initial experience of the Holy Spirit's power, and gifts. Their present enrichment of spiritual gifts was the same as, and in continuation, with their initial experience through Paul's ministry. After Paul reminds them of that past event, he immediately switches tenses to the present and acknowledges that they are currently not lacking any of the Spirit's gifts in their gatherings.

Next, he addresses their foolish notion of thinking they have 'arrived' spiritually, by switching from the present tense to the future. He tells them that now, they are not lacking any spiritual gift as they wait for the 'revealing of our Lord Jesus Christ' (1 Cor. 1:7). In other words just as God confirmed Paul's testimony to Christ to the Corinthians at the beginning through the Spirit's manifestations, so He will continue in that same manner to confirm the Corinthians to the end. Christ will continue to strengthen His church through the gifts of the Spirit until He is revealed at that last day. The Corinthians were living in an age where the Spirit was poured out, but they would one day experience a greater and fuller revelation when Christ would be revealed at His glorious coming.

Upon reading these verses, it is evident that the church should not be lacking any spiritual gifts, but experiencing the manifestation of the Spirit while she waits for the revealing of our Lord Jesus Christ.

Key Text One

'Love never ends. As for prophecies, they will pass away; as for tongues, they will cease; as for knowledge, it will pass away. For we know in part and we prophesy in part, but when the perfect comes, the partial will pass away.

When I was a child, I spoke like a child, I thought like a child, I reasoned like a child. When I became a man, I gave up childish ways. For now we see in a mirror dimly, but then face to face. Now I know in part; then I shall know fully, even as I have been fully known. So now faith, hope, and love abide, these three; but the greatest of these is love' (1 Corinthians 13:8-13).

The above puts the cessationist on the offensive. He argues that the perfect that comes is the completed New Testament - the total canon of Scripture. *'Now that we have all Scripture'* he reasons, *'tongues along with prophecy and miracles have ceased; there is no further need for their use. They helped an infant church get launched; but now that we have the Bible, we no longer require the Spirit's manifestation.'*

A sweeping statement to say the least, but is this argument credible?

One needs to bear in mind that the whole of 1 Corinthians 13 is not primarily addressing spiritual gifts. Paul's focus is on God's love. Throughout the chapter, he contrasts love with the gifts of the Spirit. *'Love never fails; God's love is perfect'* - he argues. While love will never end, (Rom. 8:38-39) the manifestation of the Spirit will. Speaking in tongues will cease, but love won't; the gift of prophecy will be no more, but love will be forever. The obvious question is *when* will these gifts cease? Paul supplies the answer - when 'the perfect' comes.

Herein lies the crux of the problem. To what or whom does 'the perfect' refer to? Cessationists state that the perfect is the complete canon of Scripture. In using Paul's analogy of a child becoming an adult, some will infer that having the complete canon, the church is now mature and in a state of adulthood in contrast with Paul's day. Believing this, they logically conclude that the Spirit's gifts are no longer for today. Such reasoning I would suggest is fundamentally flawed.

One important rule in interpreting Scripture - especially the epistles - is that whatever Scripture meant to its original writers and recipients, is what it means to us today. It cannot mean something different to us than it did when it was first written. In the case of 1 Corinthians 13:4-8, what these verses meant to Paul and the Corinthians is what they must mean to us. As Paul was writing to the Corinthians during the first century, he simply had no idea that he was writing what we call - 'The New Testament'. Such a notion was totally foreign to him, and so that being the case, it violates a principle of hermeneutics[23] to state that the phrase 'the perfect' means the completed New Testament. So what or whom exactly does 'the perfect' refer to?

---

23   Hermeneutics is the science of interpreting scripture.

Notice that Paul switches tenses[24] on two occcasions as he writes about 'the perfect'. By using the pronoun 'we' he is writing of himself and the Corinthians, and is contrasting his and their present existence with a time that is yet future. It is in this future time period that 'the perfect' will come. During Paul's time of writing, he speaks of seeing in a 'mirror dimly' and contrasts it with the future when he and the Corinthians will see 'face to face' - like looking at a reflection and looking at reality; like looking at a photograph and looking at a real person. We see this on a human level in the following:

> '*Though I have much to write to you, I would rather not use paper and ink. Instead I hope to come to you and talk face to face, so that our joy may be complete*' (2 John 12).

> '*I hope to see you soon, and we will talk face to face*' (3 John 14).

However, the phrase 'face to face' occurs on several occasions throughout the Old Testament - each time referring to seeing the Lord (Ex. 33:11; Num.14:14; Deut. 5:4; 34:10). An example is found at a defining moment in Jacob's life.

> '*So Jacob called the name of the place Peniel, saying, "For I have seen God face to face, and yet my life has been delivered"*' (Genesis 32:30).

'Face to face' in 1 Corinthians 13:12 clearly refers to one seeing the Lord. Until we see Him 'face to face', we 'walk by faith, not by sight' (2 Cor. 5:7). Cessationism

---

24   Note Paul's use of the words 'now' and 'then' to denote past and future.

states that 'the perfect' has already come, whereas the non cessationist (continuationist)[25] waits for its arrival at Christ's appearing.

Let's suppose that the cessationist is right in suggesting that 'the perfect' refers to the New Testament. Time for some probing questions.

Are we to believe that when the ink dried when the last word in the book of Revelation was written - the gifts of the Spirit ceased? Or maybe it was when the last apostle's heart stopped beating, that God withdrew all supernatural gifts. Let's probe a little further. Paul states that when *'the perfect has come, we shall know fully, even as I am fully known.'* If Paul had the complete New Testament in mind why would he speak of himself as 'knowing fully' when he wouldn't have been alive when the canon of Scripture would be recognized? Unlike Paul, we do have the complete canon of Scripture, but can we say that we know God fully as He knows us fully?

The believer is not immune from deception. Cessationists essentially are saying that because they have the New Testament, they therefore know God fully just as He fully knows them. On a personal note, I can't even know myself fully, let alone God. The cessationist's logic raises some thought provoking questions. If 'the perfect' has now come, then logically a believer should never be deceived by his or her emotions. If 'the perfect' has now come, can a Pastor by studying the Bible, be made aware if a member of his congregation is embezzling funds or committing adultery? I don't think so. Maybe that's why God has given prophetic

---

25   A continuationist is one who believes that the gifts of the Holy Spirit exist in this present age and will continue until Christ's return.

ministry to His church (1 Cor. 14:25). Can reading the Bible enable one offer prayer and praise to God directly from his or her spirit bypassing understanding. Can one always pray about people and situations objectively without prejudice and bias? Does one always know how to pray the perfect will of God in every situation? Again I would say no - hence, God gives the gift of tongues[26] (1 Cor. 14:14). Does reading the Bible alone bring physical healing?[27] Again the answer is no, so God gives gifts of healings to His church (1 Cor. 12:9). Even the most ardent skeptic should recognize the need for the gift of discerning of spirits!

In the age we live in which is rife with deception and false teaching, there is a vital need for the child of God to operate in a level of discernment. Many believers can testify of 'feeling' disturbed or uneasy when engaged in a particular conversation or walking into a certain situation. On the surface all appeared normal and as it should be, but there was an uneasiness within one's spirit. That's the Holy Spirit in us alerting and warning us to tread carefully. The Corinthians prided themselves in having 'knowledge' which Paul groups together with prophecy and tongues (1 Cor. 13:8). Therefore, if prophecy and tongues are no longer for today, then good hermeneutics would dictate that knowledge isn't either.

'…*as for knowledge, it will pass away*' (v. 8).

The term pass away is the Greek word 'katargeō' and its meaning is comprehensive. It means 'to render idle,

---

26   It is possible that Romans 8:26 refers to the gift of tongues.
27   I'm not suggesting that one cannot be healed by reading and meditating on God's word, but scripture encourages healing prayer with anointing of oil (James 5:14) and through the laying on of hands (Mark 16:18).

unemployed, inactivate, inoperative, to cause a person or thing to have no further efficiency, to deprive of force, influence, power.'[28]

Has knowledge passed away? Knowledge in this context refers to what Paul referred to as 'the message of knowledge', and if this manifestation is a teaching gift or complements a teaching gift as I have suggested, then knowledge has not passed away.

So what authority then does one have, to isolate knowledge from tongues and prophecy in the text?

There can only be one answer and that is that all the gifts of the Holy Spirit are in existence and to be exercised until Christ's appearing (1 Cor. 1:7).

It's significant to note that if 'the perfect' refers to the completed New Testament which results in gifts like speaking in tongues and prophecy ceasing, that Paul reopens the whole issue again in 1 Corinthians 14. Why doesn't the content of 1 Corinthians 14 come before 1 Corinthians 13 if he is referring to the supernatural gifts ceasing? Furthermore, if 'the perfect' refers to the canon of Scripture, why does Paul give express commands for the church to seek and pursue such gifts? (1 Cor.14:1, 39). The reason is because from Paul's perspective the gifts are not about to cease. Paul is merely instructing the Corinthian church in their use of the gifts. The Spirit's manifestation is to be facilitated, pursued and desired in a climate of *love* - hence the opening words of 1 Corinthians 14:

---

28   *www.blueletterbible.org/lang/lexicon/lexicon.
cfm?Strongs=G2673&t=KJV.*

'Pursue love, and earnestly desire the spiritual gifts, especially that you may prophesy.'

There is a clear inconsistency by many in their reading of 1 Corinthians. The majority of churches today will celebrate communion based on 1Corinthians 11 but many will reject the manifestation of the Spirit in 1 Corinthians 12 and 14.

What of the analogy of childhood and adulthood to suggest that with the complete canon of Scripture, the church is now mature? Jon Ruthven remarks that *'the Bible and orthodox doctrine were in the possession of the worst medieval popes, the driest of dead Protestant orthodoxy or liberalism, and indeed, of Satan himself!'*[29]

In conclusion, I would respectfully submit that 'the perfect' as Paul states has not yet come. 'The perfect' is Christ's appearing and not the complete canon of Scripture. I will give the last word to Dr Martin Lloyd Jones:

> *'It is perfectly clear that in New Testament times, the gospel was authenticated in this way by signs, wonders and miracles of various characters and descriptions . . Was it only meant to be true of the early church? . . . The Scriptures never anywhere say that these things were only temporary - never! There is no such statement anywhere.'*[30]

---

29   *www.hopefaithprayer.com/books/On-the-Cessation-of-the-Charismata-Ruthven.pdf*
30   Jones, Martin Lloyd. *The Sovereign Spirit: Discerning His gifts.* Harold Shaw Publishers, US 1986.

Key Text Two

'So then you are no longer strangers and aliens, but you are fellow citizens with the saints and members of the household of God, built on the foundation of the apostles and prophets, Christ Jesus himself being the cornerstone' (Ephesians 2:20).

The cessationist's argument is as follows:

The apostles and prophets have laid the foundation for God's house - i.e. the church. Their ministries, accompanied with signs and wonders are no longer required as the foundation (canon of Scripture) is now complete. In essence, when the apostles and prophets died, their gifts died with them.

As in my treatment of 1 Corinthians 13:4-8, once again I would point out the purpose of Ephesians 2:20 is not to demonstrate that the gifts of the Holy Spirit have been withdrawn, but as a plain reading of the text shows - how Gentiles, who were once separated from salvation, have now through Christ, been granted inclusion along with the Jews into 'the household of God'. The theme is equality. God's household comprising Jews and Gentiles has been built upon the foundation of the apostles and prophets, and is continually being built into a holy habitation for the Spirit (Eph. 2:21-22).

It is important to note that Christ Himself is the foundation.

> *'For no one can lay a foundation other than that which is laid, which is Jesus Christ'*
> (1 Corinthians 3:11).

Not only is Christ the foundation, He is also the 'Cornerstone'. Christ is central to this building - the church. Jesus said that He would build His church (Matt. 16:18). How does He build it? Through people - people He has gifted in various ways, all working together for a common purpose - to build God's house.

Consistency is required in interpreting this Scripture.

If, as the cessationist would argue, that the apostles and prophets together with their supernatural giftings have ceased as they were foundational, then good hermeneutics would dictate that Christ be treated in the same manner, as He too is part of the foundation. By implication, this would mean that His giftings and activities such as salvation, justification etc should also have ceased. The text states that God's house is growing in Christ and being built through the Spirit (note the present continuous tense). Paul states that the 'whole structure' is in Christ. It is taking liberty to suggest that while God's house - comprising people (Jews and Gentiles) is continually growing and being built throughout this gospel age, that the foundation (also comprising people) is somehow left in a previous time and generation if the 'whole structure' is continually being built in Christ.

In verse 20, the phrase *'having been built on the foundation of the apostles and prophets'*, according to the cessationist argument implies that apostolic and prophetic ministries, together with their ties to writing Scripture, could no longer in their view be in operation at the time of Paul's writing to the Ephesians. This is further evident, as Paul states that both Jews and Gentiles at the time of writing, have already been incorporated into the church and so metaphorically speaking, are the next layer built upon the already laid foundation of the 'apostles and prophets'. If the cessationist interpretation is correct, why then at the time of writing Ephesians, did Paul (himself being part of the foundation as an apostle) still refer to himself as an apostle (Eph.1:1), and why could he still receive and impart revelation to his readers? I would suggest the solution can only be found by disregarding the cessationist interpretation.

The following analogy may be helpful. When a person establishes a company, registers it, employs staff etc - does the founder cease to have a role? Is he still not the founder with a future role in the company? As Jack Deere says, *'the founding director of a company or corporation will always be unique in the sense that he or she was the founder, but that does not mean the company would not have future directors or presidents'.*[31]

If cessationists see no purpose today for the apostle and prophet, then what of the evangelist, pastor and teacher referred to in Ephesians 4:11? If the apostle and prophet were only for a set time, then so were the evangelist, pastor and teacher. There must be no inconsistency. It is clear from Scripture that prophets functioned in the New Testament church, and their ministry together with that of lay persons who prophesied, was not purely foundational, but to build upon the existing foundation. When Philip's daughters

---

31   Deere, Jack. *Surprised by the Power of the Spirit.* Eastbourne: Kingsway Publications, 1994, p248.

prophesied, (Acts 21:9) were they laying the once and for all foundation of the church? Was Agabus? (vv. 10-11). What about the unknown Ephesian disciples?

(Acts 19:6). A reading of Scripture will clearly show that their ministries were to strengthen and edify the people of God and not to extend the foundation already laid.

The cessationist interpretation of Ephesians 2:20 must be disregarded, as Scripture clearly states that the gift of prophecy, together with all nine manifestations of the Spirit are to be operational and expected in today's church until Christ returns (1 Cor. 1:7) - a point further reinforced by Paul:

> *'And he gave the apostles, the prophets, the evangelists, the pastors and teachers, to equip the saints for the work of ministry, for building up the body of Christ, until we all attain to the unity of the faith and of the knowledge of the Son of God, to mature manhood, to the measure of the stature of the fullness of Christ, so that we may no longer be children, tossed to and fro by the waves and carried about by every wind of doctrine, by human cunning, by craftiness in deceitful schemes.*
> *Rather, speaking the truth in love, we are to grow up in every way into him who is the head, into Christ, from whom the whole body, joined and held together by every joint with which it is equipped, when each part is working properly, makes the body grow so that it builds itself up in love'* (Ephesians 4:11-16).

Note that the ministry of the apostle and prophet, together with the evangelist, pastor and teacher, are to function until *'we all attain to the unity of the faith, and of the knowledge of the Son of God, to mature manhood unto the measure of the stature of the fullness of Christ'.* The body of Christ will not attain this expectation until Christ returns. These verses portray a glorious, mature and united people of God, which we are to aspire to become, but clearly have not yet fulfilled. Until this happens at Christ's appearing, we must endeavor to accept and acknowledge these 'five-fold' ministry gifts in the church.

Key Text Three

'Long ago, at many times and in many ways, God spoke to our fathers by the prophets, but in these last days he has spoken to us by his Son, whom he appointed the heir of all things, through whom also he created the world' (Hebrews 1:1-2).

In contrasting God speaking in the Old Covenant through the prophets with Him now speaking through His Son Jesus Christ in the New Covenant, the cessationist argues that God is no longer speaking through any prophetic avenue. 'God only speaks through His Son, and the completed canon bears testimony to Jesus, thus eliminating the gift of prophecy' the cessationist would say.

Is this a credible argument? The cessationist's argument based on Hebrews 1:1-2 is built upon a misconception that the gift of prophecy is adding to Scripture. While it is true that the Old Testament prophets were writing Scripture and their writings were included in the Old Testament canon, the New Testament gift of prophecy serves a different function. I address this under the heading 'Is prophecy adding to the bible?' in the chapter 'Common fallacies'. It's significant to note that when the book of Hebrews was written, the gift of prophecy was still in operation. If the New Testament canon renders Spiritual gifts obsolete, why then does that same New Testament command us to earnestly desire the very gifts it's supposed to have superceded? The cessationist's argument based on these verses, contradicts other Scriptures which show that the gifts of the Spirit will continue until Christ's return (1 Cor. 1:7; 13:10-12).

The Son does speak today, and He does so through Scripture, through preaching, prophecy and the gifts of the Spirit through His church.

Key Text Four

'How shall we escape, if we neglect so great salvation; which at the first began to be spoken by the Lord, and was confirmed unto us by them that heard him; God also bearing them witness, both with signs and wonders, and with divers miracles, and gifts of the Holy Ghost, according to his own will?' (Hebrews 2:3-4).

The writer of Hebrews states that signs and wonders confirmed the gospel preached by *'them that heard Him'*. Cessationists interpret this verse to mean that signs and wonders were done by the apostles (or those associated with them), as they heard Jesus firsthand and witnessed His ministry; therefore signs and wonders do not occur today following gospel preaching because no one today has heard and witnessed Jesus' ministry firsthand.

This reasoning is flawed. It is inaccurate to say that it was only the apostles who heard and witnessed Jesus' ministry firsthand, as Scripture records many others who did also. At least seventy others heard Christ (Luke 10:1) as did approximately five hundred at His ascension (1 Cor. 15:6). Furthermore cessationists are propagating an argument from silence. The verse in question does not say that those who hadn't heard Jesus could not have had signs and wonders confirming their preaching of the gospel.

An important further point should be noted, namely that the writer to the Hebrews makes a distinction between signs, wonders and various miracles, with gifts of the Holy Ghost. Consistency is once again called for because if signs and wonders were confined only to the apostles, then the 'gifts of the Holy Ghost' must be as well. As stated before, Paul did not foresee the gifts of the Holy Spirit confined to operating in a limited time frame, but actually continuing until Christ's return.

> *'Now you have every spiritual gift you need as you eagerly wait for the return of our Lord Jesus Christ'* (1 Corinthians 1:7) (NLT).

Common Fallacies

1. Prophesying is Adding to the Bible

This common objection arises from a misunderstanding of the definition and working of the New Testament gift of prophecy. Many sincere believers equate the New Testament gift of prophecy with the ministry of the Old Testament prophet. Herein lies the confusion.

Consider the Old Testament prophet. Whenever he spoke he was speaking with Divine authority and the words which he spoke and wrote were the very words of God. Such prophetic utterances were characterized by wordings such as *'thus says the Lord'*! Any individual who gave a prophetic utterance which failed to come to pass was stoned, as the Lord's Name was dishonoured. When the Old Testament prophets were writing God's words they were writing Scripture, and Timothy states that such writings were inspired or God-breathed (2 Tim.3:16).

Contrast with the New Testament gift of prophecy.

Phenomena such as dreams, visions, impressions and hearing an audible voice come under the umbrella of New Testament prophecy. Remember, the argument of the cessationist is that exercising the gift of prophecy is tantamount to adding to Scripture.

How then can the New Testament gift of prophecy be defined?

Consider Paul's remarks:

> '*Two or three prophets should speak, and the others should weigh carefully what is said. And if a revelation comes to someone who is sitting down, the first speaker should stop. For you can all prophesy in turn so that everyone may be instructed and encouraged* (1 Corinthians 14:29-31).

The keywords in the above verses are *revelation* and *speak*. Prophecy is simply speaking a revelation; it is communicating something which has been revealed. Prophets were in the Corinthian church and they were speaking/prophesying to the believers. The scenario was that if something was revealed to someone, that individual would signal to the one prophesying to conclude, so he could communicate his 'revelation'. The moment someone began speaking what had been revealed to him - he was *prophesying*. It's important to note that the New Testament uses the term 'revelation' on occasions which do not result in written scripture or words equal to scripture in authority (Matt.11:27; Rom 1:8; Eph 1:17; Phil. 3:15).

Prophesying is simply the act of speaking forth what God has revealed.

What is a revelation? It's simply something that the Holy Spirit impresses upon one's mind or spirit. It could be a dream, a vision or a Scripture. Many preachers have experienced either before or during the delivery of a sermon, a fresh insight or understanding of a Scripture, and they knew they had to share it with their congregation. Surely that was a manifestation of the Holy Spirit - God revealing something to be communicated. How many preachers upon sharing such a spontaneous insight had someone come up to them later and relate how that truth greatly encouraged and ministered to them in their situation? Was that the gift of prophecy? I believe so on two accounts. Firstly it is communicating something which God has revealed, and secondly it brings edification, exhortation and comfort which Paul says is the purpose of prophecy (1 Cor. 14:3). If such an experience can happen spontaneously to a preacher in preparation and in the pulpit, why can it not also happen on a one to one basis during prayer or counseling? Couldn't the one praying or counseling be given a Scripture or a 'mini sermon' just for the individual they are ministering to?

Unfortunately many have moved away from the simplicity of this powerful gift and won't acknowledge a prophetic utterance unless it is prefaced and concluded with *'thus says the Lord'*. Prophecy is a gift the church is encouraged to seek after and its potential is great. When one grows in this gift, (Rom.12:6) it is possible to become a vessel which God can use, not only to encourage others, but to disclose the very secrets of the hearts of people (1 Cor. 14:24-25) and so bring glory to Himself.

Once again, note the contrast between the Old Testament prophet and the New Testament gift of prophecy as shown by the following.

In Acts 21:4 Paul was implored by his fellow disciples who were speaking through the Spirit (prophetically) not to go to Jerusalem. If Paul considered the New Testament gift of prophecy to be equal to prophetic utterances spoken by an Old Testament prophet, he would never have disobeyed, because to do so would have meant disobeying God.

In 1 Corinthians 14:30, Paul permitted prophesying to be interrupted - something which would be unthinkable in the Old Testament. He also recognized that those in Corinth who were speaking prophetically were *not* speaking the very words of God.

> *'Or was it from you that the word of God came?'*
> (1 Corinthians 14:36).

It is apparent that the Old Testament prophet and the New Testament gift of prophecy are very different. As stated earlier, the Old Testament prophet spoke with Divine authority and His words were the very words of God. Old Testament prophets were also given authority to write Scripture. New Testament prophets did not write Scripture. In the New Testament, anyone who spoke prophetically was communicating what he or she sensed God to be saying.

The exercise of the gift of prophecy has a margin for error, hence the command to test and evaluate all that purports to be prophetic.[32] While the gifts are perfect, they are exercised through imperfect vessels. Nowhere in the New Testament is it assumed that the utterances of a prophet or the exercise of the gift of prophecy are tantamount to writing Scripture or adding to the Bible. It must be pointed out also that the gift of prophecy is not just preaching in itself as many wrongly assume. The New Testament Greek text has two distinct words for prophesying and preaching. If prophesying and preaching were the same, then Paul would not have permitted women to prophesy. Although he seems to have allowed women to prophesy, (1 Cor. 11:5) he prohibited them from preaching, (1 Tim. 2:12) which

---

32   Sermons should also be tested and evaluated (1 Thess. 5:21).

underscores the fact that prophesying and preaching are understood to be different and not the same.

The church needs encouragement and Paul saw the gift of prophecy as a means to provide it. Every believer can participate in this vein and is encouraged to do so (1 Cor. 14:39).

2. Why do People who have 'The Gift of Healing' not go and empty Hospital Wards?

Those who use the above to justify the non-existence of healing gifts today, reveal a basic ignorance of Scripture. All gifts of the Spirit are exercised under the sovereign operation of God (1 Cor. 12:4-6; 11). The operation of prophetic gifts is under the sovereignty of the Spirit and cannot be turned on and off like a tap,[33] and neither can gifts of healings.

In John 5 when Jesus went to the pool of Bethesda, He healed just one person. Here in the midst of a multitude of sick people, Jesus healed just one. A multitude is a lot and yet Jesus didn't empty this 'hospital'. Why?

Several verses later we find the answer:

> 'So Jesus said to them, "Truly, truly, I say to you, the Son can do nothing of his own accord, but only what he sees the Father doing. For whatever the Father does, that the Son does likewise"' (John 5:19).

If Jesus operated by this principle, then why should His followers be expected to heal at will?

---

33   Note the word 'if' in 1 Corinthians 14:27.

Paul demonstrated gifts of healings, but clearly could not heal at will.[34] Some will argue that Paul couldn't bring healing to his friends Trophimus and Timothy, because 'the gift of healing' was beginning to diminish and wane. This argument is weak because later in Paul's life when he was shipwrecked on Malta, God used him to heal the father-in-law of Publius and also others on the island who were sick (Acts 28:8-9).

People who pray for the sick are wrongly described as having 'the gift of healing'. In 1 Corinthians 12:9 there is the absence of the definite article. Within the body of Christ, are 'gifts of healings'. A person said to have 'the gift of healing' suggests a high success rate in praying for healing for all kinds of sicknesses. Such a mentality can dissuade many believers from praying for the sick because if they haven't seen any results, they conclude they don't have 'the gift of healing'. However, if we understand that there are 'gifts of healings' in the body of Christ, then every one of us can be used by God in healing, even if we see just one person or many healed in our lifetimes. Whether we see only certain or many kinds of sicknesses healed or whether we see healing administered through individual laying on of hands or en masse through corporate prayer, the scope for healing is wide and varied.

We need to ask God and expect Him to use us in 'gifts of healings' when compassion rises within us to minister to the sick and afflicted. I would like to stress a further point about healing and that is regarding the use of medicine. God heals today! He heals supernaturally and through natural means. Doctors and nurses are on the side of healing and I strongly

---

34   It is probable that Trophimus and Timothy weren't healed through Paul's ministry (2 Tim.4:20; 1Tim. 5:23).

advocate medical care.[35] I believe that prayer enhances medical care even to the point of accelerating what's considered to be a normal, expected speed of recovery.

3. Speaking in Tongues is the Ability to Preach the Gospel in a Foreign Language

How I wish! Such a remark often stems from an underlying motive which seeks to discredit speaking in tongues today.

> *'For one who speaks in a tongue speaks not to **men** but to God; for no one understands him, but he utters mysteries in the Spirit'* (1 Cor. 14:2) (Emphasis mine).

Note the phrase *'for no one understands him'.* Speaking in tongues as described in the above Scripture is clearly not confined to a known human language. It should also be stated that speaking in tongues is not directed towards man, but towards God.

Those who claim that the use of the gift of tongues is to enable one to preach the gospel in a foreign language, appeal to the day of Pentecost for justification. The reality is no one *preached* in other tongues on Pentecost, but rather *praised* God in other tongues. Upon hearing tongues, the onlookers were amazed, but upon hearing Peter's sermon in his own native language, they were convicted of their sin. Later in Peter's life, in response to a vision, and a request of a centurion called Cornelius, he traveled to visit him in Caesarea. While Peter preached in Cornelius' home, the Holy Spirit fell upon Cornelius and his invited friends and as a result, they spoke in tongues and magnified God. My question is that if the gift of tongues is given for the purpose

---

35   My wife Rosnah is a medical doctor.

of preaching the gospel in a foreign language not previously learned, then who were Cornelius and the new believers in his house preaching to when they spoke in tongues? (Acts 10:46).

If speaking in tongues enables one to communicate in a known language, then logically, it's for the benefit of those who hear the message. Why then, if tongues are a known language does Paul spend much time praying in tongues in private where there is no one to hear him? (1 Cor. 14:18-19).

Suppose speaking in tongues is speaking in a known language. According to Ethnologue, there are 6909 known living languages.[36] To claim that speaking in tongues is not for today, or to dismiss it as gibberish, would require one to be a linguistic expert with a knowledge of all 6909 languages for such a claim to stand.

The gift of tongues like the others in 1 Corinthians 12 is relevant for today. It is invaluable in the believer's prayer-life by edifying and enabling the believer to pray when words fail or seem to be inadequate. It should never though be worn as a badge of superiority, but rather recognized as an invaluable help in our frailty and weakness. Paul held this gift in high regard and encourages the believer to seek God for it (1 Cor. 14:5, 18).

4. The Greek Text Infers that the Gift of Tongues will Cease, Before the Lord's Return.

While some cessationists concede that prophecy and knowledge will vanish at the Lord's return, they will appeal to the structure of the Greek text to suggest that tongues

---

36   *www.ethnologue.com.*

could cease at any time independently of knowledge, prophecy and Christ's coming again. Their rationale is predicated on the fact that the Greek verb used with knowledge and prophecies is in the passive voice, whereas the verb used with tongues is in the middle voice. Greek verbs are made up of five elements: Person, Number, Tense, Mood and Voice. This argument centres on 'Voice', which describes the relationship of a verb with its subject. There are three such 'voices', namely 'Active', 'Passive', and 'Middle' which furnish the argument in question. In the active voice, the subject performs the action of the verb whereas in the passive, the subject receives the action of the verb. In the middle voice, the subject participates in the results of the verb. In the case of tongues, the verb 'cease' is in the middle voice, suggesting that tongues can cease by themselves independently of knowledge, prophecy which were caused to cease by the Lord's return.

Don Carson however points out that *'when Jesus rebukes the wind and raging waters, the storm stops (same verb, middle-voice in Luke 8:24) - and certainly not under its own power.'*[37] The verb 'ceased' in Luke 8:24 though in the middle voice was contingent upon Jesus' command. The storm certainly did not cease by itself. We see another example in Acts 19:28-41; 20:1.

The Early Church's impact on society began to unsettle the silversmiths of Ephesus. Unrest began to breed among them which spread throughout the city leading to a potential riot and perhaps even fatalities. Luke records that the whole city was in confusion (Acts.19:29) and a sea of people swept Paul's traveling companions into the theatre. Mounting

---

37   Carson, D.A. *Showing the Spirit.* Grand Rapids: Baker Books, 1987, p67.

tensions brought the intervention of the town official and a sense of normality ensued. It's significant to note that the uproar of the crowd in Ephesus ceased upon the threat of a town official. Again the verb 'ceased' is in the middle voice, but once again, the uproar didn't cease by itself.

While at first glance the argument of the 'middle voice' seems impressive, it can not serve as conclusive scriptural evidence of the gift of tongues ceasing at any moment.

5. Tongues is Ecstatic Speech!

The word 'ecstatic' suggests a state of ecstasy, and implies that one speaking in tongues is perhaps out of control or in a frenzied or trance-like state and oblivious to his surroundings. Scripture clearly demonstrates, that the tongues-speaker is in control and can start and stop speaking at will (1 Cor. 14:15-19, 32). Consider the following:

> 'If any speak in a tongue, let there be only two or at most three, and each in turn, and let someone interpret' (1 Cor. 14:27).

Paul envisages the tongues-speaker retaining control, hence the command that speaking in tongues in the church be limited to only two or three persons at most. Paul writes this in a context where there was loud unfettered speaking in tongues en masse, which led to confusion and the potential of outsiders charging such a church as being *'out of your minds'* (1 Cor. 14:23).

6. The Gifts of the Spirit were given only to the Apostles because they wrote Scripture.

Firstly, the gifts of the Spirit were not only given to the apostles. Scripture records Philip who wasn't an Apostle, being used in the working of miracles (Acts 8:6). Stephen, the first Christian martyr (Acts 6:8) was also used in doing mighty miracles. There was an unknown individual who cast out demons which was considered a miracle by Jesus (Mark 9:38-39). Both the Corinthian (1 Cor. 12:10) and Galatian (Gal. 3:5) churches were experiencing miracles. None of the above examples wrote Scripture, so the premise that the gifts of the Spirit were only given to the Apostles to authenticate their ministry and writing of Scripture is inaccurate.

It's significant to note also that Paul makes a distinction between apostles and those who exercised the gift of the working of miracles.

> *'And God has appointed in the church first apostles, second prophets, third teachers, then miracles, then gifts of healing, helping, administrating, and various kinds of tongues'* (1 Cor. 12:28).

Factors to Consider

I believe that many people who do not call themselves Pentecostal or Charismatic have experienced the gifts of the Spirit operating in their lives. Consider Charles Haddon Spurgeon known as 'the Prince of Preachers'. What follows is an experience he had while preaching. He was preaching in Exeter Hall when during the sermon he stopped and pointed in a certain direction and said:

> *'"Young man, those gloves you are wearing have not been paid for: you have stolen them from your employer." At the close of the service, a young man, looking very pale and greatly agitated, came to the room which was used as a vestry, and begged for a private interview with Spurgeon. On being admitted, he placed a pair of gloves upon the table, and tearfully said, "It's the first time I have robbed my master, and I will never do it again. You won't expose me, sir, will you? It would kill my mother if she heard that I had become a thief." The preacher had drawn the bow at a venture, but the arrow struck the target for which God intended it, and the startled hearer was, in that singular way, probably saved from committing a greater crime.*[38]

---

38   *www.cblibrary.com/biography/spurgeon/spurg_v2/spau2_04. htm.*

*P*entecostals would call this a 'word of knowledge' while Spurgeon probably would not. Many feel uncomfortable with Pentecostal terminology so maybe it's merely a question of semantics, and if so, then there are possibly those who consider themselves to be cessationists in principle, but in experience, may not be.

What Spurgeon related was clearly a supernatural operation of the Holy Spirit and was not an isolated incident. Consider the following:

'A man living in Newington had been converted through the Pastor's preaching and he became a regular worshipper at the Tabernacle. His wife, a very staunch member of the Church of England, strongly objected to his going, but he continued to attend notwithstanding all that she said.

One Sabbath night, after her husband had gone to the service, her curiosity overcame her prejudice, and she herself determined to go to hear what the preacher had to say. Not wishing to be known, she tried to disguise herself by putting on a thick veil and a heavy shawl, and sought still further to avoid observation by ascending to the upper gallery. She was very late in reaching the building, so, just as she entered, the preacher was announcing his text, and the first words that sounded in her ears were strikingly appropriate to her case, especially as she declared that Spurgeon pointed directly at her as he said, "Come in, thou wife of Jeroboam; why feignest thou thyself to be another? For I am sent to thee with heavy tidings" (1 Kings 14:6.)

This singular coincidence further impressed her when, in the course of his sermon, the Pastor said: "While thus speaking about the occasional hearer, an idea haunts my mind that I have been drawing somebody's portrait. I think there are some here who have had their character and conduct sketched out quite accurately enough for them to know who is meant. Do remember that, if the description fits you, it is meant for you; and if you yourself have been described, do not look about among your neighbours and say, "I think this is like somebody else." If it is like you, take it home to yourself, and God send it into the centre of your conscience, so that you cannot get rid of it!...

... I do not suppose there is anybody here disguised as to dress tonight, though such things may happen. The working man, who is afraid he shall be laughed at if he be known, may come here in disguise. Now and then a clergyman may come in, who would not be very comfortable in his conscience if it were known he did such a thing, and so he does not show himself exactly in his wonted garb. Notwithstanding, whoever you may be, disguised or not, it is of no use where God's gospel is preached. It is a quick discerner, and will find out the thoughts and intents of the heart. It will search you out, and unmask your true character, disguise yourself as you may."

When the husband reached home, the woman revealed her secret, and said that he must, somehow, have let Spurgeon know that she was up in the gallery of the Tabernacle. The good man assured her that he was quite innocent, but she would not be convinced. The next day, when he saw the Pastor, he told him what a hard time he was having through his wife's singular experience the previous evening.[39]

It is occurrences like these which confirm the Bible's teaching on continuationism. I would venture to say that the young man and woman (who were profoundly affected by

---

39   *www.cblibrary.com/biography/spurgeon/spurg_v2/spau2_04. htm.*

these separate, supernatural occurrences), would probably be instilled with a passion and fear of Almighty God as a result.

The body of Christ needs more of such happenings, not just for the sake of them, but to edify and encourage as the Lord in His sovereignty grants them. One prominent Bible teacher stated that 'the gifts of the Spirit are tools - not toys.' Any workman knows that the tools of his trade must be handled and operated with great care and expert precision.

We need to strive for excellence in ministry.

A Climate of Love

Sandwiched between 1 Corinthians 12 and 14 is a chapter on God's love. Contrary to popular belief, love is not cited as a gift but is the motivation for God's gifts. Paul describes the pathway of love as a 'more excellent way' (1 Cor. 12:31). The church of Jesus Christ must strive for excellence. We are ambassadors for the most High God and so must ensure that our conduct reflects and represents Him accurately. While the gifts of the Spirit are given by God's grace, I believe they should be ministered in excellence.

Donald Gee *'challenged unbelief and the traditions of man but also corrected fanaticism and warned against error'.*[40]

Consider healing. There must be sensitivity to and compassion for the sick; uplifting and encouraging them with God's word. The sick must not go away under a weight of condemnation and guilt. We live in an age where miracles are marketed to generate interest in healing ministries. Whether the motives are pure or impure is not

40   Malcomson, Keith. *Pentecostal Pioneers Remembered.* Maitland: Xulon Press, 2008, pp343-344.

for me to say, but it's all too common for someone to claim a healing success, only to find that the facts are not what they seem. If we strive for excellence then we will ensure that healing is not discredited and brought into disrepute. Before trumpeting a healing or a miracle, investigative measures ought to be undertaken. A genuine healing can and should be medically verified and such verification will inspire faith and encourage others.

Like healing, the gift of prophecy has also been abused. In healing, many sick have been pronounced healed when they are not and many have left feeling condemned for a lack of faith, believing their sickness is their fault. Abuse has crept into prophetic ministry. Many have entered into marriages purely on the basis of a prophecy. There is no attraction, no mutual love, but because the man or woman of God has said *'thus says the Lord'* many sincere couples have plunged into unhappy marriages. Excellence in ministry demands accountability. Earlier in this book, I pointed out that Scripture requires all prophecy to be subject to testing. If someone prophesies but that prophecy does not come to pass, then there needs to be an admission of error. Servants of God must be accountable.

> *'Do not quench the Spirit. Do not despise prophecies, but test everything; hold fast what is good'* (1 Thessalonians 5:19-21).

It's significant that when Paul seeks to establish order in the Corinthian church, he's concerned for the effect its disorder will have on unbelievers and the ungifted (those who are unaccustomed to the Spirit's dynamic in a gathering of believers).

'Even so, if unbelievers or people who don't understand these things come into your church meeting and hear everyone speaking in an unknown language, they will think you are crazy. But if all of you are prophesying, and unbelievers or people who don't understand these things come into your meeting, they will be convicted of sin and judged by what you say' (1 Corinthians 14:23-24) (NLT).

If believers are misusing the Spirit's gifts and are giving themselves to fleshly behaviour, unbelievers and those who are unaccustomed or uninformed, will label them as 'mad'! By contrast, if everything is being done decently and in order, the unbeliever will be convicted of his sin, and the uninformed will see the power of the Spirit at work, and desire such gifts to be manifest in his own life.

Why Speak in Tongues?

It goes without saying that speaking in tongues can be perceived as being controversial. It's an emotive issue amongst many believers, with some extolling its benefits thus embracing it while others shun it. Some say because it is the manifestation which Paul cites last, it is therefore the least of all the gifts. The reason why Paul cites it last, is merely because it was this gift which was being misused and misunderstood. Paul addressed the problem and administered correction, while at the same time encouraged its continued use in both individual and corporate capacities. The gift of tongues is of immense benefit to the child of God. It is praying with one's spirit, and it brings edification particularly in the private devotional life.

> *'For if I pray in a tongue, my spirit prays but my mind is unfruitful'* (1 Corinthians 14:14).

> *'One who speaks in a tongue edifies himself; but one who prophesies edifies the church'* (v. 4) (NASB).

To edify means to build up. Speaking in tongues enables one to be built up spiritually. It helps build spiritual muscle. While believers are corporately being built up when they meet together as a local church, they need ongoing edification daily. Scripture demonstrates that tongues are used in prayer and praise.

Praying in tongues bypasses the mind in that it is the believer's spirit praying and not his understanding.

> '*For if I pray in a tongue, my spirit prays but my mind is unfruitful*' (v. 14).

At times we don't know how to pray, what to pray and don't even feel like praying. Here God has graciously given to His church, a wonderful gift to build us up when we are feeling weak, and so enable us pray the perfect will of God, free from all bias and prejudice as we speak mysteries in the Spirit (v. 2).

Not only is this gift used for prayer, but also for praise. On the day of Pentecost, the onlookers heard one hundred and twenty believers praise and magnify God in different languages. Paul even spoke of singing in other tongues (v. 15).

Paul himself esteemed this gift very highly. He thanked God that he spoke in tongues more than all the Corinthians did. He did not forbid its use (v. 39), but instead encouraged every believer in the Corinthian church to speak in tongues (v. 5).

God has created us to know Him and fellowship with Him. Why not avail of this wonderful gift of tongues to help in prayer and praise?

Are the Gifts of the Spirit Really Necessary?

Some may ask: 'Is it really important whether or not one believes that the Holy Spirit's manifestations are for today?'

In response to such a valid question, I submit the following. Firstly, the Holy Spirit plays such a key role in the worship context. He glorifies Jesus Christ! (John 16:14). In the worship setting, He should be expected to manifest Himself through the body of Christ in diverse ways, and His ministry should be facilitated (1 Cor. 12:7). He manifests Himself so that the people of God will profit. Paul who wrote 1 Corinthians under the inspiration of the Holy Spirit acknowledged that what He wrote were the commandments of the Lord (1 Cor. 14:37). In that vein, he said to *earnestly desire to prophesy and do not forbid speaking in tongues'* (v. 39).

He encouraged the believers to pursue love and to *desire* spiritual gifts, especially prophecy (v. 1). Most today are faithful to pursue love, but perhaps equally unfaithful to desire spiritual gifts, especially prophecy. The command to 'desire' in relation to spiritual gifts is the Greek word 'ζηλόω' (zēloō)[41] which means to burn with zeal. In other

---

41   *www.blueletterbible.org/lang/lexicon/lexicon. cfm?Strongs=G2206&t=KJV.*

words it means to be 'red hot'. Are we 'red hot' in our quest for the gifts of the Spirit to operate in our lives, ministries and churches? Does that describe our zeal for the Spirit to manifest Himself? Dr Craig Keener makes a valid point in asking *'would God place such commands in Scripture if they were relevant for only four decades, especially since during most of that time the majority of ancient Christians would not have yet had access to Paul's letter?'*[42]

The Corinthian church had many problems such as carnality, immorality, drunkenness, believers initiating lawsuits and some even denying Christ's resurrection. However, in spite of all these problems, this church had spiritual gifts in abundance. God's power was at work. There was such an abundance of spiritual gifts, that tongues and prophecy were being misused. How would modern pastors address such misuses? Perhaps they would understandably 'tone things down' or even suspend the exercise of such gifts. Paul's approach was quite different. His solution was not prohibition, but correction. He tells them to keep desiring spiritual gifts, especially prophecy and not to forbid speaking in tongues (1 Cor. 14:39). Given the misuse of tongues and prophecy, and the problems in the Corinthian church, and that Paul acknowledged he was writing the commandments of the Lord (v. 37), his imperative to the church to desire spiritual gifts and not to forbid speaking in tongues, reveals the heart of God on these important issues.

God wants His people when they assemble for worship to make room for, and experience the fulness of His Spirit for their edification, exhortation and comfort. In practical terms this means each believer being an instrument for

---

42 Keener, Craig S. *Gift and Giver: The Holy Spirit for Today.* Grand Rapids: Baker Academic, 2001, p107.

the Holy Spirit to flow through for the benefit of others. Scripture makes a distinction between being *filled* with the Spirit and being *full* of the Spirit. Being filled with the Spirit is for the purpose of a temporary outward work as the need arises, whereas being full of the Spirit is a permanent internal work - a state of being.

Examples of being filled with the Spirit are as follows:

> '*And they were all filled with the Holy Ghost, and began to speak with other tongues, as the Spirit gave them utterance*' (Acts 2:4).

When the 120 persons in the Upper room were filled with the Holy Spirit on the day of Pentecost, they spoke in other tongues. Afterwards Peter preached a powerful message which resulted in 3000 coming to repentance and faith.

> '*Then Peter, filled with the Holy Spirit, said to them, "Rulers of the people and elders, if we are being examined today concerning a good deed done to a crippled man, by what means this man has been healed, let it be known to all of you and to all the people of Israel that by the name of Jesus Christ of Nazareth, whom you crucified, whom God raised from the dead - by him this man is standing before you well. This Jesus is the stone that was rejected by you, the builders, which has become the cornerstone. And there is salvation in no one else, for there is no other name under heaven given among men by which we must be saved." Now when they saw the boldness of Peter and John, and perceived that they were uneducated, common men, they were astonished. And they recognized that they had been with Jesus*' (Acts 4:8-13).

When Peter and John were brought before Caiaphas and the High Priest for questioning, Peter was filled with the Holy Spirit and began to speak boldly to them. Note Peter's boldness: '*…let it be known to all of you and to all the people of Israel that by the name of Jesus Christ of Nazareth, whom you crucified, whom God raised from the dead… This Jesus is the stone that was rejected by you…*'

Peter was filled with the Spirit to enable and empower him speak the word of God boldly to the religious leaders. What an amazing contrast, when we consider that this was the same man who had denied Jesus!

Upon release, Peter and John returned to their own company where Peter began to pray. When he had finished praying, the room shook as they were all filled again with the Holy Spirit which resulted in them speaking the word with boldness (Acts 4:31).

Scripture demonstrates that being filled with the Holy Spirit is for a temporary outward work as the need arises such as preaching, praising, praying and prophesying.

Being full of the Holy Spirit describes a continual inner condition where He works within, purifying and purging us to reveal Christ in and through us. Examples can be seen as follows:

> '*Therefore, brothers, pick out from among you seven men of good repute, **full** of the Spirit and of wisdom, whom we will appoint to this duty*' (Acts 6:3) (Emphasis mine).

> '*for he was a good man, **full** of the Holy Spirit and of faith. And a great many people were added to the Lord*' (Acts 1:24)(Emphasis mine).

Being *full* of the Spirit creates godly character and a climate for the fruit of the Spirit to flourish.

As Roger Helland points out: *'Filling is about gifting. Fulness is about holiness.'*[43]

> *'But you will receive power when the Holy Spirit has come upon you, and you will be my witnesses in Jerusalem and in all Judea and Samaria, and to the end of the earth'* (Acts 1:8).

The Holy Spirit grants power to believers to be witnesses for Jesus Christ and I would suggest that the power He gives, both transforms us and reveals Christ in us, as well as flows through us to work miracles, heal the sick and speak prophetically etc.

In Acts 16:23-34, when the earthquake shattered the prisoners' chains in the Philippian prison which culminated in the household salvation of the jailer, I wonder how the Holy Spirit arrested his attention and brought him to his knees. Did the Spirit speak to him through the earthquake, or perhaps was it through Paul and Silas not attempting to escape? The Holy Spirit is given to reveal Christ in us and to empower us to do His works.

I would suggest that there are three biblical principles one can adopt in cultivating both the presence and power of the Holy Spirit. Firstly, we need to ask God. Wanting God's character and power in our lives is scripturally valid. James reminds us that we have not because we ask not (James 4:2). However as James cautions, it is imperative that we

---

43   Helland, Roger. *The Revived Church*. Tonbridge, Kent: Sovereign World Ltd, 1998, p56.

check our motives (v. 3). Why do we want God's power and presence in our lives? Is it so that we can look good and be admired and praised, or is it so that Jesus will be glorified? May our motives be pure so that we will decrease, and He will increase (John 3:30). Our asking must be fuelled by a desire. We must not merely ask for the sake of asking, but we must truly see the necessity of revealing Christ in and through our lives by word and deed (fruit and gifts).

Thirdly, there must be a willingness to yield. When we learn to sense the Holy Spirit prompting and prodding us to action, we must obey. As we demonstrate obedience, He acts. These principles are needed in our pursuit of holiness. When one desires to live a holy life, that desire will be expressed in prayer driven by the necessity to honour God and reveal Christ. Then there will inevitably be opportunities for the individual to yield to the Spirit's prompting. When the Spirit speaks one makes the decision to either obey or disobey; to act either in accordance with God's word or succumb to 'the flesh'. This is equally true when it comes to demonstrating the power of God through the gifts of the Spirit. Recognizing its importance one will express such a desire in prayer. I believe doors of opportunity will then be open (to witness or pray for the sick or prophesy) to those sincerely seeking such.

In our quest for the Spirit's manifestation, we must not forget that we are to desire gifts and not purchases. They cannot be earned as they are bestowed by God's grace. However, our willingness to be used can cost us, as spiritual gifts operate in the will of God, and doing the will of God at times can be costly especially in terms of misunderstanding. Remember though, that the rewards vastly outweigh the cost.

Summary

When one received the Holy Spirit in the New Testament, it was a dynamic experience. People knew they had received. John the Baptist spoke of a 'baptism in the Holy Spirit' (Matt. 3:11). Consider the setting in which John proclaimed *'I baptize you with water for repentance, but he who is coming after me is mightier than I, whose sandals I am not worthy to carry. He will baptize you with the Holy Spirit and fire.'*

John immersed repentant sinners in the River Jordan. As he plunged them under the waters and hoisted them up again, he, in effect, said that what he did for them in water, Jesus would do for them in the Holy Spirit. Those who would be baptized in the Holy Spirit and fire, would be immersed into the presence of God, and they would be plunged into His power and purified by His fire. The fulfilment of this occurred on the day of Pentecost and was presupposed for believers from then onwards (Acts 2:38-39; 1 Cor. 12:13). Jesus had spoken beforehand to expect this outflow after His glorification (John 7:37-39).

People spoke in tongues, some prophesied and others boldly proclaimed the message of Christ. Receiving the Spirit was not merely inferred because one believed in Christ, but was an event one could point to. It was an experience which brought the power of God into their lives and a greater degree of intimacy with God.

Consider Romans 5:5:

> *'and hope does not put us to shame, because God's love has been poured into our hearts through the Holy Spirit who has been given to us.'*

God's love has been poured out into the believer's heart by the Holy Spirit. The love of God in this verse refers to God's love for the believer as opposed to the believer's love for God. His love is poured into the believer's heart. This is significant as the heart is the seat of emotions, the arena of the mind, feelings and intellect. When God's love by His Spirit, is poured into the believer's heart, it affects and touches the emotions and feelings. It is a subjective experience. The child of God feels God's love. He or she experiences God's presence. Not only is Romans 5:5 an objective truth, but it is also a subjective experience. It's important to note that we don't live by experience and feelings, but there are times when God does things in our lives to remind us of and affirm His love for us.

God's love poured into the believer's heart by the Spirit is a subjective experience. The question is: Do cessationists allow the believer to expect and experience such an individual outpouring of God's love today?

While Romans 5:5 speaks of God's love for us being poured out in our hearts, Galatians 4:6 speaks of the Spirit birthing intimacy for God within us:

> *'And because you are sons, God has sent the Spirit of his Son into our hearts, crying, "Abba! Father!"'*

The same Holy Spirit who pours out God's love into our hearts, also births within us such a desire to love God,

81

which expresses itself in our crying out *'Abba Father'*. This was the same intimate language which Jesus used to speak to the Father in the garden of Gethsemane (Mark 14:36). The Holy Spirit is given to enable us know God intimately and experience His love and presence.

> *'For through him we both have access in one Spirit to the Father'* (Ephesians 2:18).

Paul desired to know Christ intimately and He acknowledged the Holy Spirit's role in this. The power responsible for raising Christ from the dead, provided the basis for intimacy with the Lord.

> *'that I may know him and the power of his resurrection, and may share his sufferings, becoming like him in his death'* (Philippians 3:10).

Will the cessationist permit or deny the dynamic role of the Spirit in the believer's loving relationship with God? Experiencing the presence of the Spirit not only cultivates intimacy with God which leads to a sensitivity to His voice, but also paves the way for His power. Sensitivity to His voice and the release of His power are expressed through the Spirit's gifts.

Paul in 1 Corinthians 1:7 shows the time-frame for the activity of the gifts of the Spirit. The Corinthians were not to be lacking in any gift as they waited for the revealing of Christ at His coming. He reinforces this time-frame by telling us in 1 Corinthians 13:12 that the gifts of the Spirit will eventually cease, when we see our glorious Lord and Saviour face to face. While the gifts of the Spirit are temporary, God's love is eternal. However one does not know the expiration date on these gifts as no one knows the day or hour of the Lord's return when the temporal gives way to the eternal.

Perhaps as you have read this short treatise, a desire for the gifts of the Spirit has been awakened within. Maybe you have been taught the doctrine of cesssationism, but now are questioning its tenets. God knows the sincerity of both the hearts of cessationists and continuationists. Let God have His way in your life as you seek answers and make yourself an available vessel for Him to use to bless others for His glory.

As individual believers and as the body of Christ, let's seek for and expect God's Spirit to manifest Himself powerfully in and through our lives for the glory of His Son Christ Jesus. However, we must ensure in our seeking, that gifts don't take priority over the Giver. We must seek God as a priority, and seek Him because of who He is and not only so that we can avail of His gifts.

My prayer is that you, the reader will be fully convinced that the Spirit's manifestations outlined in 1 Corinthians 12 and 14 are necessary for today and that you will begin to experience them in your own life as you take your place in fulfilling the Great Commission.

A Way Forward

As you approach the end of this book, your paradigm may be challenged and long standing views shaken. I pray that as you reflect upon and contemplate what has been written, that the Holy Spirit will reveal the important truth of His manifestations today and impel you to desire them.

Maybe the issue has already been settled and you have come to see that cessationism has no scriptural foundation. If so, what next? Well, if you belong to a church which acknowledges and facilitates the ministry of the Spirit, then you are perfectly poised to learn and exercise whatever gift or gifts the Spirit will give you. But what if you are in a church which does not advocate the continuing supernatural ministry of the Spirit?

Consider the following words of Jesus:

> *'No one puts a piece of unshrunk cloth on an old garment, for the patch tears away from the garment, and a worse tear is made. Neither is new wine put into old wineskins. If it is, the skins burst and the wine is spilled and the skins are destroyed. But new wine is put into fresh wineskins, and so both are preserved'* (Matthew 9:16-17).

Old wine skins are hard and easily torn, and cannot accommodate new fermenting wine. New fermented wine housed in an old wineskin would ultimately burst it. A new wine skin by contrast is elastic and flexible to stretch with the new fermenting wine as it brings expansion. This illustration in its original context shows how the ministry of Jesus could not be poured into the old wineskin of Judaism.

Respectfully, many churches today have inflexible formal structures in place that simply cannot accommodate the new wine of the Spirit in all its fulness. If you, the reader, have experienced or are ready to experience the Spirit's power and gifts, but belong to a church which has structures akin to old wineskins, then out of respect for the leadership in that church, you should not pursue your desire for spiritual gifts there. What you can do is pray for your church that there will be a hunger for, and receptivity to the Holy Spirit's fulness. In addition, I would encourage you to attend, perhaps, a mid-week Pentecostal or 'Full Gospel'[44] prayer meeting or bible study to keep your new found flame of the Spirit burning, and to provide you with an opportunity to develop your gifts.

May God bless you and lead you on this exciting pathway as you seek to honour and glorify the name of our Lord and Saviour Jesus Christ.

---

44   By this I mean churches/fellowships which embrace the gifts of the Spirit as outlined in 1 Cor.12: 8-10.

Appendix:
Blasphemy against the Holy Spirit

To blaspheme the Holy Spirit creates fear in many sincere believers. For some ministers and leaders of movements, it is used as ammunition to warn (threaten?) those who question their doctrine and practices. Sincere believers live in despair believing they are guilty of committing this offence. But what exactly is blaspheming the Holy Spirit?

> *'And whoever speaks a word against the Son of Man will be forgiven, but whoever speaks against the Holy Spirit will not be forgiven, either in this age or in the age to come'* (Matthew 12:32).

It is essential that we understand the role 'context' plays in establishing what this unforgivable sin is.

When Jesus spoke the above words, He was physically on earth. People could see Him, hear Him and touch Him. Folks could observe His conduct and the mighty works that God did through Him. Having seen these and then knowingly attribute the works of Christ to the power of Satan was blasphemy. Jesus is no longer here on earth physically, so the context changes somewhat. It would be akin today to wilfully and deliberately attributing the work of a servant of Christ who is graciously used to do signs and wonders through the power of the Holy Spirit, as being the work of Satan.

Blasphemy against the Holy Spirit is not a remark made in ignorance. Paul admitted that he was a blasphemer, but obtained mercy, because he did it out of ignorance and unbelief (1 Tim.1:13). To blaspheme the Holy Spirit is a willful act which merits no forgiveness.

Consider Mark's rendering of Jesus' words:

> '*but whoever blasphemes against the Holy Spirit never has forgiveness, but is guilty of an eternal sin*' (Mark 3:29).

According to Mark's Gospel the one who blasphemes the Holy Spirit will *never* experience forgiveness - not just of this sin, but any sin. Consider what Jesus says prior to this remark.

> '*Truly, I say to you, all sins will be forgiven the children of man, and whatever blasphemies they utter*' (v. 28).

Jesus says that *all* sins and *all* blasphemies will be forgiven. Note the word '*all*'.

How are *all* sins and blasphemies forgiven? The answer is by confessing them.[45]

What are we to conclude from this? Those who blaspheme the Holy Spirit will never experience forgiveness, because they will never truly confess that sin. They will not be convicted in their conscience and so will never confess any sins, and receive forgiveness and cleansing. Their conscience

---

45   1 John 1:9 includes all sins and blasphemies.

will be so seared and their heart calloused that they will not be aware of their sin.

There is hope for the troubled and tormented who believe they have crossed a line with blasphemy written on it; minds that are tormented and in turmoil, racked with worry and anxiety, wanting God, but fearful that it's too late.

Dear friend, why would the Holy Spirit create within you a desire for God (Rom. 8:15; Gal. 4:6) and make you aware of sin if you had blasphemed Him? If you truly were guilty of blaspheming Him, He would be so wounded that never again would He allow you to sense God's love and presence.

The one who blasphemes the Holy Spirit doesn't even know it nor could care less.

Dear friend, rejoice in the goodness and grace of God who bought you with the precious blood of His beloved Son. You were bought with a price; you were washed in the blood of Jesus, clothed in His righteousness and sealed with His Holy Spirit. God has stamped His ownership upon you. He calls you His child.

Bibliography

Carson, D.A. *Showing the Spirit*. Grand Rapids: Baker Books, 1987.

Deere, Jack. *Surprised by the Power of the Spirit*. Eastbourne: Kingsway Publications, 1994.

Gee, Donald. *Concerning Spiritual Gifts*. Springfield: Gospel Publishing House, 1980.

Grudem, Wayne. *Systematic Theology*. Leicester: Inter-Varsity Press, 1994.

Helland, Roger. *The Revived Church*. Tonbridge, Kent: Sovereign World Ltd, 1998.

Hillstrom, Elizabeth L. *Testing the Spirits*. Downers Grove: InterVarsity Press, 1995.

Keener, Craig S. *Gift and Giver: The Holy Spirit for Today*. Grand Rapids: Baker Academic, 2001.

Malcomson, Keith. *Pentecostal Pioneers Remembered*. Maitland: Xulon Press, 2008.

Mullin, Robert Bruce. *Miracles and the Modern Religious Imagination*. New Haven: Yale University Press, 1996.

Nañez, Rick M. *Full Gospel, Fractured Minds?: A Call to Use God's Gift of the Intellect.* Grand Rapids: Zondervan, 2005.

Storms, Sam. *The Beginner's Guide to Spiritual Gifts.* Ventura: Regal Books, 2002.

Electronic Sources

Calvin, John. 'Institutes of the Christian Religion'. *Book IV Chapter 19.* www.spurgeon.org/~phil/calvin/bk4ch19.html.

'Catholic Encylopedia' *www.newadvent.org/cathen/05716a.htm*

'Blue Letter Bible Lexicon'. *Blue Letter Bible. www.blueletterbible.org.*

Ethnologue, Languages of the World. www.ethnologue.com.

Ruthven, Jon Mark. 'On the Cessation of the Charismata: The Protestant Polemic on Post-Biblical Miracles'. www.hopefaithprayer.com/books/On-the-Cessation-of-the-Charismata-Ruthven.pdf

'The Autobiography of Charles Spurgeon'. *Spurgeon Autobiography, Volume 2, Chapter 4. www.cblibrary.com/biography/spurgeon/spurg_v2/spau2_04.htm.*

About the Author

Mark Anderson has been involved in a preaching and teaching ministry since 1990, mainly to churches and fellowships within the United Kingdom. He has also taught the Word of God in Southern Ireland, Malaysia, Ukraine and Sri Lanka. Apart from his role as a church elder, he is a member of International Gospel Outreach (IGO).

Mark lives in County Armagh, Northern Ireland with his wife Rosnah and their three children, Joanna, Zoe and Zachary.

He can be contacted at the following address:

Lisnadill Full Gospel Church
Ballymoran Road
Armagh
Co Armagh
BT60 2AW
N Ireland
Email: info@markanderson.org.uk
Website: www.markanderson.org.uk